Cycling
in
SOUTH WALES
& THE WYE VALLEY
Seiclo yn Ne Cymru ac yn Nyffryn Gwy

Published by Collins
An imprint of HarperCollins*Publishers*
77–85 Fulham Palace Road
London W6 8JB

www.**fire**and**water**.com
www.bartholomewmaps.com

First published 2001
Copyright © HarperCollins*Publishers* Ltd 2001
Maps © Bartholomew Ltd 2001

Collins® is a registered trade mark of
HarperCollins*Publishers* Limited

Routes compiled by the following:
Martin Brain, Howard & Mary Hynam, Graham Mills, Kirsty Morris (CTC Cymru);
Richard Harries (Cardiff DA); Chris Buck (Cerridigion DA); Des James (Chester & North Wales DA);
Helen Gilmour (Shropshire & Mid Wales DA); Mike Evans, Des Radford (Swansea & West Wales DA);
Sandra Shaw.

Design by Creative Matters Design Consultancy, Glasgow.
Typeset by Bob Vickers.

Photographs reproduced by kind permission of the following:
Cadw: Welsh Historic Monuments, Crown Copyright, page 37; Forest Enterprise page 37;
Herefordshire Tourism page 8; Wales Tourist Board pages 5, 11, 14, 20, 25, 27, 50, 53, 55,
63, 67, 71, 74, 79, 89, 99, 108.

The Publisher makes no representations or warranties of any kind as to the
operation of the web sites listed in this guide, and disclaims all responsibility
for the content of the web sites and for any expense or loss incurred by use
of the web sites.

The landscape is changing all the time. While every care has
been taken in the preparation of this guide, the Publisher accepts
no responsibility whatsoever for any loss, damage, injury or
inconvenience sustained or caused as a result of using this guide.

The Publishers welcome comments from readers. Please address your letters to:
Collins Cycling Guides, HarperCollins Cartographic, HarperCollins Publishers,
Westerhill Road, Bishopbriggs, Glasgow, G64 2QT.

Printed in Singapore

ISBN 0 00 710375 1
01/1/12

CONTENTS

KEY TO ROUTES

Distances have been rounded up or down to the nearest 0.5km (mile).

Route colour coding

undemanding rides compiled specifically with families in mind
16.5–29km (10.5–18 miles)

middle distance rides suitable for all cyclists
29–40km (18–25 miles)

half-day rides for the more experienced and adventurous cyclist
40–70km (25–43.5 miles)

challenging full-day rides
over 70km (over 43.5 miles)

grande randonnée – a grand cycling tour
over 100km (60 miles)

 Routes marked with this symbol are off-road or have off-road sections
(includes well-surfaced cycleways as well as rougher off-road tracks)

The Black Mountains

LOCATION MAP

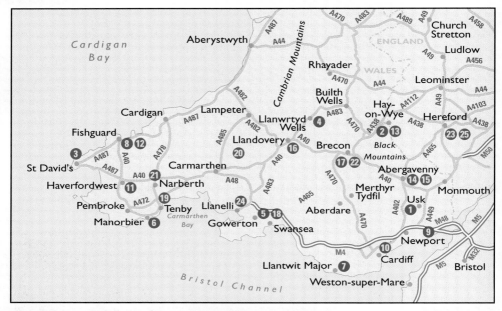

KEY TO ROUTE MAPS

⟨M23 Service area A259⟩	Motorway
A259	'A' road / Dual carriageway
B2130	'B' road / Dual carriageway
	Good minor road
	Minor road
	Track / bridleway
●━━	Railway / station
	Canal / river / lake
- - - - - - -	Ferry route
50	Contour (height in metres)

	Cycle route / optional route
🚲	Start of cycle route
⑫—	Route direction
Ⓑ	Place of interest
🍵	Public house
☕	Café / refreshments
✕	Restaurant
🍲	Convenience store
i	Tourist Information Centre
Ⓟ	Parking

☎	Telephone
⊼	Picnic site
▲	Camping site
👫	Public toilets
†	Place of worship
⚘	Viewpoint
⚑	Golf course
⁘	Tumulus
	Urban area
	Woodland

Height above sea level

50	100	150	200	300	400	500	600	700	800	900 metres
165	330	490	655	985	1315	1645	1975	2305	2635	2965 feet

INTRODUCTION

How to use this guide

Collins' *Cycling in South Wales & the Wye Valley* has been devised for those who want trips out on their bicycles along quiet roads and tracks, passing interesting places and convenient refreshment stops without having to devise their own routes. Each of the 25 routes in this book has been compiled and ridden by an experienced cyclist for cyclists of all abilities.

Cycling in Cycling in South Wales & the Wye Valley is easy to use. Routes range from undemanding rides compiled specifically with families in mind to challenging full-day rides; the type of route is easily identified by colour coding (see page 5). At the start of each route an information box summarises: total distance (in kilometres/miles — distances have been rounded up or down throughout to the nearest 0.5km/mile and are approximate only); grade (easy, moderate or strenuous based on distance and difficulty); terrain; an average time to allow for the route; directions to the start of the route by car and, if appropriate, by train.

Each route is fully mapped and has concise, easy-to-follow directions. Comprehensive information on places of interest and convenient refreshment stops along each route are also given. Accumulated mileages within each route description give an indication of progress, while the profile diagram is a graphic representation of gradients along the route. These should be used as a guide only.

The following abbreviations are used in the route directions:

LHF	left hand fork
RHF	right hand fork
LHS	left hand side
RHS	right hand side
SO	straight on
SP	signpost
TJ	T junction
TL	turn left
TR	turn right
XR	crossroads

Cycling in South Wales & the Wye Valley

The area covered by this guide contains two national parks (the Pembrokeshire Coast and the Brecon Beacons) and Britain's first designated Area of Outstanding Natural Beauty, the Gower Peninsula. As well as spectacular coastline and mountain ranges, there are ancient standing stones and burial mounds, the remnants of Roman roads and numerous castles, many constructed by the Normans after their invasion of Britain in 1066. Much of the traditional heavy industry has disappeared but some of the disused pits and buildings have been converted into visitor centres. The River Wye rises just outside the area covered by this guide, on the slopes of Plynlimon in the Cambrian Mountains. It flows to Rhayader, Builth Wells and Hay-on-Wye, before running through the picturesque area known as the Wye Valley, to Ross-on-Wye, Monmouth and Chepstow.

Some of the routes use sections of the National Cycle Network, which is being developed by the charity Sustrans, with the help of a £43.5 million grant from the Millennium Commission. Two National Cycle Routes cross Wales: the Celtic Trail (NCR 4/47), Lôn Geltaidd, from Fishguard through south Wales to Chepstow; and the Welsh National Route (NCR 42/8), Lôn Las Cymru, from Cardiff and Chepstow north across country to Holyhead. A third route is planned across north Wales, between Chester and Holyhead. Numerous routes, both on- and off-road, are administered by the Forestry Commission and local councils. For further information on the National Cycle Network write to Sustrans, 35 King Street, Bristol, BS1 4DZ, telephone (0117) 926 8893, or visit their website at www.sustrans.org.uk

Preparing for a cycling trip

Basic maintenance

A cycle ride is an immense pleasure, particularly on a warm sunny day. Nothing is better than coasting along a country lane gazing over the countryside. Unfortunately, not every cycling day is as perfect as this, and it is important to make sure that your bike is in good order and that you are taking the necessary clothing and supplies with you.

Before you go out on your bicycle check that everything is in order. Pump the tyres up if needed, and check that the brakes are working properly and that nothing is loose – the brakes are the only means of stopping quickly and safely. If there is a problem and you are not sure

Hereford Cathedral

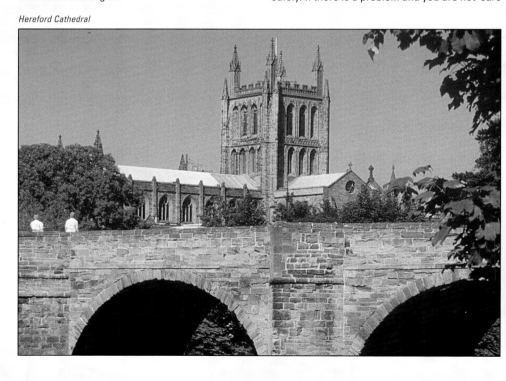

that you can fix it, take the bike to a cycle repair shop – they can often deal with small repairs very quickly.

When you go out cycling it is important to take either a puncture repair kit or a spare inner tube – it is often quicker to replace the inner tube in the event of a puncture, though it may be a good idea to practise first. You also need a pump, and with a slow puncture the pump may be enough to get you home. To remove the tyre you need a set of tyre levers. Other basic tools are an Allen key and a spanner. Some wheels on modern bikes can be removed by quick release levers built into the bike. Take a lock for your bike and if you have to leave it at any time, leave it in public view and locked through the frame and front wheel to something secure.

What to wear and take with you
It is not necessary to buy specialised cycling clothes. If it is not warm enough to wear shorts wear trousers which are easy to move in but fairly close to the leg below the knee – leggings are ideal – as this stops the trousers catching the chain. If you haven't got narrow-legged trousers, bicycle clips will hold them in. Jeans are not a good idea as they are rather tight and difficult to cycle in, and if they get wet they take a long time to dry. If your shorts or trousers are thin you might get a bit sore from being too long on the saddle. This problem can be reduced by using a gel saddle, and by wearing thicker, or extra, pants. Once you are a committed cyclist you can buy cycling shorts; or undershorts which have a protective pad built in and which can be worn under anything. It is a good idea to wear several thin layers of clothes so that you can add or remove layers as necessary. A zip-fronted top gives easy temperature control. Make sure you have something warm and something waterproof.

If you wear shoes with a firm, flat sole you will be able to exert pressure on the pedals easily, and will have less work to do to make the bicycle move. Gloves not only keep your hands warm but protect them in the event that you come off, and cycling mittens which cushion your hands are not expensive. A helmet is not a legal require-ment, but it will protect your head if you fall.

In general it is a good idea to wear bright clothing so that you can be easily seen by motorists, and this is particularly important when it is overcast or getting dark. If you might be out in the dark or twilight fit your bicycle with lights – by law your bicycle must have a reflector. You can also buy reflective bands for your ankles, or to wear over your shoulder and back, and these help motorists to see you.

You may be surprised how quickly you use up energy when cycling, and it is important to eat a carbohydrate meal before you set out. When planning a long ride, eat well the night before. You should eat small amounts of food regularly while you are cycling, or you may find that your energy suddenly disappears, particularly if there are hills or if the weather is cold. It is important to always carry something to eat with you – chocolate, bananas, biscuits – so that if you do start fading away you can restore yourself quickly. In warm weather you will sweat and use up fluid, and you always need to carry something to drink – water will do! Many bicycles have a fitment in which to put a water bottle, and if you don't have one a cycle shop should be able to fit one.

It is also a good idea to carry a small first aid kit. This should include elastoplasts or bandages, sunburn cream, and an anti-histamine in case you are stung by a passing insect.

It is a good idea to have a pannier to carry all these items. Some fit on the handlebars, some to the back of the seat and some onto a back rack. For a day's ride you probably won't need a lot of carrying capacity, but it is better to carry items in a pannier rather than in a rucksack on your back. Pack items that you are carrying carefully – loose items can be dangerous.

Getting to the start of the ride

If you are lucky you will be able to cycle to the start of the ride, but often transport is necessary. If you travel there by train, some sprinter services carry two bicycles without prior booking. Other services carry bicycles free in off-peak periods, but check the details with your local station. Alternatively, you could use your car – it may be possible to get a bike in the back of a hatchback if you take out the front wheel. There are inexpensive, easily fitted car racks which carry bicycles safely. Your local cycle store will be able to supply one to suit you.

Cycling on-road

Cycling on back roads is a delight with quiet lanes, interesting villages and good views. The cycle rides in this book are mainly on quiet roads but you sometimes cross busy roads and have stretches on A and B roads, and whatever sort of road you are on it is essential to ride safely. Always be aware of the possibility or existence of other traffic. Glance behind regularly, signal before you turn or change lane, and keep to the left. If there are motorists around, make sure that they have seen you before you cross their path. Cycling can be dangerous if you are competing for space with motor vehicles, many of which seem to have difficulty in seeing cyclists. When drivers are coming out of side roads, catch their eye before you ride in front of them.

You will find that many roads have potholes and uneven edges. They are much more difficult to spot when you are in a group because of the restricted view ahead, and therefore warnings need to be given. It is a good idea to cycle about a metre out into the road, conditions permitting, so that you avoid the worst of the uneven surfaces and to give you room to move in to the left if you are closely overtaken by a motor vehicle.

Other things to be careful of are slippery roads, particularly where there is mud or fallen leaves. Sudden rain after a period of dry weather often makes the roads extremely slippery. Dogs, too, are a hazard because they often move unpredictably, and sometimes like to chase cyclists. If you are not happy, stop or go slowly until the problem has passed.

Pedalling

Many modern bikes have 18 or 21 gears with three rings at the front and six or seven on the back wheel, and for much of the time you will find that the middle gear at the front with the range of gears at the back will be fine. Use your gears to find one that is easy to pedal along in so that your feet move round easily and you do not put too much pressure on your knees. If you are new to the bike and the gears it is a good idea to practise changing the gears on a stretch of flat, quiet road so that when you need to change gears quickly you will be ready to do so.

Cycling in a group

When cycling in a group it is essential to do so in a disciplined manner for your own, and others', safety. Do not ride too close to the bicycle in front of you – keep about a bicycle's length between you so that you will have space to brake or stop. Always keep both hands on the handlebars, except when signalling, etc. It is alright to cycle two abreast on quiet roads, but if it is necessary to change from cycling two

Strumble Head

abreast to single file this is usually done by the outside rider falling in behind the nearside rider; always cycle in single file where there are double white lines, on busy roads, or on narrow and winding roads where you have a restricted view of the road ahead. Overtake on the right (outside) only; do not overtake on the inside.

It is important to pass information to other members of the group, for example:

car up – a vehicle is coming up behind the group and will be overtaking;

car down – a vehicle is coming towards the group;

single up – get into single file;

stopping – stopping, or

slowing/easy – slowing due to junction, etc., ahead;

on the left – there is an obstacle on the left, e.g. pedestrian, parked car;

pothole – pothole (and point towards it).

Accidents

In case of an accident, stay calm and, if needed, ring the emergency services on 999. It is a good idea to carry a basic first aid kit and perhaps also one of the commercial foil wraps to put around anyone who has an accident to keep them warm. If someone comes off their bicycle move them and the bike off the road if it is safe to do so. Get someone in the party to warn approaching traffic to slow down, and if necessary ring for an ambulance.

Cycling off-road

All the routes in this book take you along legal rights of way – bridleways, byways open to all traffic and roads used as public paths – it is illegal to cycle along footpaths. Generally the off-road sections of the routes will be easy if the weather and ground are dry. If the weather has been wet and the ground is muddy, it is not a good idea to cycle along bridleways unless you do not mind getting dirty and unless you have a mountain bike which will not get blocked up with mud. In dry weather any bicycle will be able to cover the bridleway sections, but you may need to dismount if the path is very uneven.

Off-road cycling is different to cycling on the road. The average speed is lower, you will use more energy, your riding style will be different and there is a different set of rules to obey – the off-road code:

1 Give way to horse riders and pedestrians, and use a bell or call out to warn someone of your presence.

2 Take your rubbish with you.

3 Do not light fires.

4 Close gates behind you.

5 Do not interfere with wildlife, plants or trees.

6 Use only tracks where you have a right of way, or where the landowner has given you permission to ride.

7 Avoid back wheel skids, which can start erosion gulleys and ruin the bridleway.

Some of the off-road rides take you some miles from shelter and civilisation – take waterproofs, plenty of food and drink and basic tools – especially spare inner tubes and tyre repair equipment. Tell someone where you are going

and approximately when you are due back. You are more likely to tumble off your bike riding off-road, so you should consider wearing a helmet and mittens with padded palms.

Useful contacts

Cycling organisations
CTC – see page 119
Sustrans – see page 8

Cycling websites
Online resources for cyclists in the UK
www.cyclecafe.com

Internet bicycling hub
www.cyclery.com

Information and support for cyclists in the UK
www.cycleweb.co.uk

Cycling information station
www.cycling.uk.com

Cycle touring in Wales & the Welsh Borders
www.kc3.co.uk/-bicycle/sideways

Local cycle hire
Abergavenny Mountain Bike Hire
3 Cross Street, Abergavenny
Telephone (01873) 850910

Brooks Cycles
9 Severn Street, Welshpool
Telephone (01938) 553582

Builth Wells Cycles
Smithfield Road, Builth Wells
Telephone (01982) 552923

Chepstow Cycles
1 St Mary Street, Chepstow
Telephone (01291) 626126

Cyfartha Visitor Centre
Brecon Road, Merthyr Tydfil
Telephone (01685) 376940

Haven Sports
Marine Road, Broadhaven
Telephone (01437) 781354

Taff Trail Cycle Hire
Cardiff Caravan Park, Cardiff
Telephone (02920) 398362

Also local cycle shops (see below).

Local cycle shops
Brecon Cycle Centre
9 Ship Street, Brecon
Telephone (01874) 622651
www.breconcycles.zx3.net

Cycles Irfon
Beulah Road, Llanwrtyd Wells
Telephone: (01591) 610710
www.cyclesirfon.co.uk

Mike's Bikes
17 Prendergast, Haverfordwest
Telephone (01437) 760068

Paddles & Pedals
15 Castle Street, Hay-on-Wye
Telephone (01497) 820604

Tourist information
Wales Tourist Board
Telephone (02920) 499909
www.visitwales.com

Abergavenny Tourist Information Centre
Telephone (01873) 857588

Brecon National Park Information Centre
Telephone (01874) 623156

Cardiff Tourist Information Centre
Telephone (02920) 227281

Chepstow Tourist Information Centre
Telephone (01291) 623772

Crickhowell Tourist Information Centre
Telephone (01873) 812105

Fishguard Tourist Information Centre
Telephone (01348) 874737

Hay-on-Wye Tourist Information Centre
Telephone (01497) 820144

Haverfordwest Tourist Information Centre
Telephone (01437) 763110

Hereford Tourist Information Centre
Telephone (01432) 268430

Llandovery Tourist Information Centre
Telephone (01550) 720693

Llanelli Tourist Information Centre
Telephone (01554) 772020

LLanwrtyd Wells Tourist Information Centre
Telephone (01591) 610666

Merthyr Tydfil Tourist Information Centre
Telephone (01685) 379884

Monmouth Tourist Information Centre
Telephone (01600) 713899

Narberth Tourist Information Centre
Telephone (01834) 860061

Pembroke Tourist Information Centre
Telephone (01646) 622388

Ross-on-Wye Tourist Information Centre
Telephone (01989) 562768

St Davids National Park Centre
Telephone (01437) 720392

Swansea Tourist Information Centre
Telephone (01792) 468321

Tenby Tourist Information Centre
Telephone (01834) 842404

Local councils
Carmarthenshire Council
Telephone (01267) 234567
www.carmarthenshire.gov.uk

Hereford Council
Telephone (01432) 260261
www.herefordshire.gov.uk

Monmouthshire Council
Telephone (01633) 644853
www.monmouthshire.gov.uk

Pembrokeshire Council
Telephone (01437) 764551
www.pembrokeshire.gov.uk

Vale of Glamorgan Council
Telephone (01446) 700111
www.valeofglamorgan.gov.uk

Public transport information
UK Public Transport Information
www.pti.org.uk

National Travel Hotline
Telephone (09065) 500000

Travel by rail
National Train Enquiries Line
Telephone (08457) 484950

Railtrack
www.railtrack.com

Central Trains
Telephone 0121 654 1200
www.centraltrains.co.uk

First Great Western
Telephone (08457) 000125
www.greatwesterntrains.co.uk

The Train Line
www.thetrainline.com

Valley Lines
Telephone (02920) 449944
www.valleylines.co.uk

Virgin Trains
Telephone (08457) 222333

Wales & West
Telephone (02920) 430090
www.walesandwest.co.uk

Weather forecasts
BBC Weather
www.bbc.co.uk/weather

The Met. Office
Telephone 09003 406 108
www.met-office.gov.uk

UK Weather Links
www.ukweather.links.co.uk

Youth Hostels Association of England and Wales
Telephone (01727) 855215
www.yha.org.uk

USK AND TREDUNNOCK

Route information

Distance 16.5km (10.5 miles)

Grade Easy

Terrain Well-surfaced, quiet roads. The route is generally flat, except for one gentle climb into Tredunnock.

Time to allow 1–2 hours.

Getting there by car Usk is on the A472 and A449, approximately 12.5km (8 miles) north east of Pontypool. There is plenty of parking in the town.

Getting there by train There is no practical railway access to this ride.

This route takes you through the peaceful Monmouthshire countryside. From Usk, the route heads south through the Usk Valley to Tredunnock, where the route turns north and follows another quiet road back to Usk.

Places of interest along the route

🅐 Usk

A small, bustling market town, with many fine Georgian buildings, originally built on the site of the Roman fort *Burrium*. Picturesque Tywn Square is overlooked by the ruins of **Usk Castle**, a medieval fortress built above the River Usk to guard the river crossing. The castle is privately owned but visitors can explore the gardens and castle ruins on open days in June; by appointment at other times. Telephone (01291) 672563. **Gwent Rural Life Museum**, New Market Street, is situated in an old malt barn and describes local history from Victorian times through to World War II. Open April to October, Monday–Friday 1000– 1700, weekends 1300–1700. Charge. Telephone (01291) 673777; www.visitwyevalley.com

Usk Valley

Food and drink

Plenty of choice in Usk and country pubs passed en route. There is a convenience store in Llangybi. In Llanbadoc, behind the church, there is a pleasant picnic area beside the river.

White Hart Inn, Llangybi
Pub serving tea, coffee and bar meals.

Newbridge Inn, Newbridge on Usk
Country pub and restaurant with a riverside garden.

Greyhound Country Inn, between Llantrisant and Llanllowell
Pub and restaurant serving a variety of meals.

Route description

Leave Usk via river bridge at west end of main street. TL, SP Caerleon. Continue into Llanbadoc.

1 SO through village and continue on this road through Llangybi, to foot of hill just beyond village.

2 TL, no SP but just before Court Bleddyn Hotel (6.5km/4 miles). Follow road as it rises to XR, where TL and continue into Tredunnock.

3 SO through Tredunnock for steep descent (CARE) and good views into hamlet of Newbridge. Continue across river.

4 TL at TJ, SP Usk (9.5km/6 miles). Continue into Llantrisant.

5 Arrive Llantrisant (11km/7 miles). TR by first houses and take lane through centre of village. At end of village TR at bus shelter and

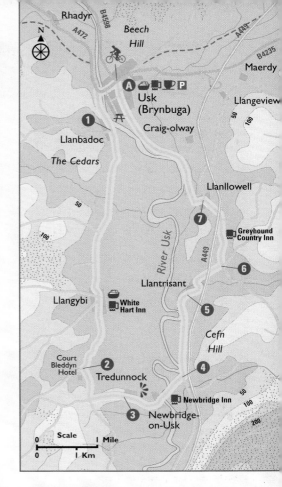

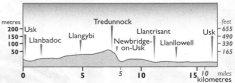

pass under road bridge. Continue for a steep rise to TJ.

6 TL at TJ.

7 Continue SO through Llanllowell (13.5km/8.5 miles), and along this road into Usk to finish the ride. ***16.5km (10.5 miles)***

2 HAY-ON-WYE AND DORSTONE

Route information

Distance 19km (12 miles)

Grade Moderate

Terrain Quiet minor roads with one long climb into Dorstone. The extended route includes a steep climb, suitable for bicycles with low gears.

Time to allow 1–3 hours.

Getting there by car Hay-on-Wye is 24km (15 miles) north east of Brecon on the B4350 (toll bridge) and B4348. There is a car park in the town, by the Tourist Information Centre.

Getting there by train There is no practical railway access to this route.

An attractive circuit from Hay-on-Wye on the Welsh/English border, along quiet country roads to Dorstone. The route can be extended to take in Brewardine (total distance 32km/ 20 miles, allow 2–4 hours).

Places of interest along the route

A Hay-on-Wye

A market town situated on the River Wye, famous for its second-hand and antiquarian bookshops and known as the Town of Books – there are some 30 bookshops in the town and a book festival is held each May. There are also many craft shops and galleries. The town is popular with outdoor enthusiasts – it is at the northernmost point of the Brecon Beacons National Park, close to the Black Mountains, on the route of Offa's Dyke long distance path and the National Cycle Network. Also scenic riverside walks. The ruins seen in the town centre are the remains of a 12th-century castle. Contact the Tourist Information Centre for more information (see page 13); www.hay-on-wye.co.uk

B Brewardine

On the extended route, Brewardine is a peaceful village on the banks of the River Wye. The bridge over the river dates from the 18th-century and was the only bridge in the area to survive floods in 1795. The village is known as the home and burial place of the 19th-century diarist Francis Kilvert, who was rector of Brewardine for just two years.

C Arthur's Stone, near Dorstone

An ancient burial chamber on Dorstone Hill. There are fine views over the Golden Valley. English Heritage property. Free access at all reasonable times. Telephone (01793) 414926; www.english-heritage.org.uk

D Dorstone

An attractive village centred on the village green. The church dates from the 19th-century but is though to be on the site of an earlier 13th-century church, said to have been built by Richard de Brito to atone for his part in the murder of Thomas Becket. The Pandy Inn is the oldest inn in Herefordshire and is also thought to have been built by Richard de Brito to house the workers building the church.

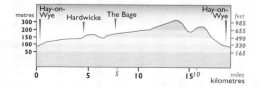

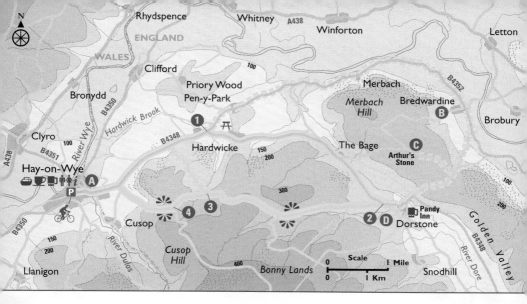

Route description

TR out of car park onto B4348. Cycle out of Hay-on-Wye and continue on this road into Hardwicke.

1 To extend the route, SO onto B4352, SP Brewardine. Follow this road through Brewardine. Pass TR (near top of climb) for Arthur's Stone. Continue and descend (with CARE). TR at TJ onto B4348, no SP. Continue past church. TL to cycle through Dorstone and join main route at direction 2, where TL, SP Mynddbrith.

Otherwise, TR to stay on B4348, SP Dorstone (picnic area on LHS). Steep climb ahead.

2 To visit Dorstone and Pandy Inn, TL, SP Dorstone.

Otherwise, to continue route, TR, SP Mynddbrith, for a long steady climb and descent with panoramic views across Herefordshire. ***14.5km (9 miles)***

3 To avoid more climbs, SO, SP Archenfield. Descend and TL at TJ onto B4348, no SP. Continue into Hay-on-Wye to finish the ride.

Otherwise, to continue main route, TL, SP Cusop/Hay-on-Wye, and climb.

4 TR at TJ, SP Hay-on-Wye (16.5km/10.5 miles). Make long descent (with excellent views across Wye Valley). TL at TJ onto B4348, no SP. Continue into Hay-on-Wye and finish the ride. ***19km (12 miles)***

Food and drink

Plenty of cafés, pubs and convenience stores in Hay-on-Wye.

 Pandy Inn, Dorstone
Bar meals served. Open every lunchtime except Monday.

ST DAVID'S AND MIDDLE MILL

Route information

Distance 20km (12.5 miles)

Grade Easy

Terrain Well-surfaced, quiet narrow lanes and a stretch of A road which can be busy in summer.

Time to allow 2–3 hours.

Getting there by car St David's is on the A487, approximately 24km (15 miles) from Fishguard and Haverfordwest. Park in the car park by the National Park Visitor Centre (signposted).

Getting there by train There is no practical railway access to this route.

A short circuit in Pembrokeshire, which has the country's only coastal national park. From St David's the route heads east to the hamlet of Middle Mill. From here the route turns north and then west to circuit back to St David's with marvellous views. An optional extension (total distance 28km/17.5 miles, allow 3–4 hours) takes you on through St David's to Porth Clais and St Justinians on the coast.

Route description

TR out of National Park Visitor Centre car park onto A487, no SP. Continue and pass school on LHS.

1 TL immediately after school, no SP.

2 TR at TJ, no SP. Continue on this road and descend into Middle Mill. **6.5km (4 miles)**

3 TR over bridge, no SP. Then TR at TJ, SP Llandeloy. Take first TL, no SP, and climb.

4 TL at XR, no SP. Continue on this road for short, steep descent with sharp bend at the bottom, then a climb.

5 TL onto A487, no SP and immediately TR (CARE), no SP (9km/5.5 miles). Continue on this road, with excellent views on RHS.

6 TL, no SP (where road bends to right). More views.

7 TR to visit Rhosygihwen Dairy Tearooms.

Otherwise, to continue route, TL at TJ, no SP.

8 TR no SP (14.5km/9 miles).

9 TL no SP.

10 SO over B4583 at XR (16.5km/10.5 miles). Continue for approximately 1km (0.6 mile).

11 Bear L into cathedral precincts. Bear L again and dismount. Walk across footbridge and continue past cathedral (below on L). See directions below to visit Porth Calais/St Justinians or continue through St David's and follow SP back to Visitor Centre and the end of the ride. **20km (12.5 miles)**

To visit Porth Calais and St Justinians:

12 TL in city centre after war memorial, SP Porth Clais. Continue into Porth Clais and follow road round to right.

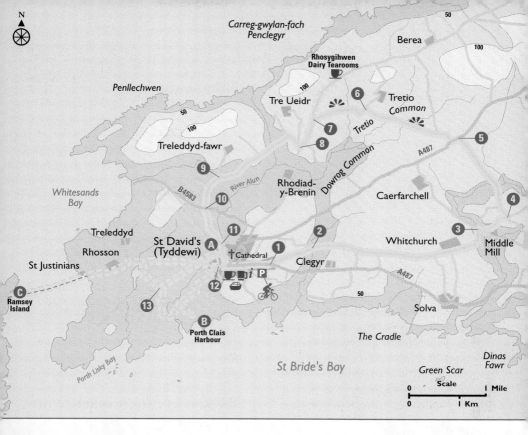

13 To visit St Justinians (boat trips to Ramsey Island), SO at XR. Then TL at TJ and continue to St Justinians.

Otherwise, to continue route, TR at XR and follow road back into St David's, where TR and follow SP Visitor Centre to finish the ride.

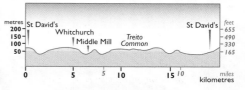

Places of interest along the route

Ⓐ St David's

An ancient cathedral city, considered to be Britain's smallest. It is named after the patron saint of Wales, St David, who founded a monastery here in the 6th century. During the 12th century **St David's Cathedral** was built on

the site of the monastery, in a hollow to protect it from attack. The Normans fortified the building and enclosed all the cathedral buildings within walls. The cathedral is in regular use as a place of worship and a venue for concerts. Open all year, daily 0800–1800; cathedral shop open Monday–Saturday during summer. Donation requested. Telephone (01437) 720247; www.stdavidscathedral.org.uk. Adjacent to the cathedral are the remains of the **Bishop's Palace**, built between 1328 and 1347 and, at the time, one of the most impressive medieval palaces in Wales. Much of the palace was destroyed during the 16th century but the remains allow visitors to appreciate the scale of the building. Cadw property. Open daily 0930–1800 (closes earlier outside summer, telephone to confirm). Charge. Telephone (01437) 720517; www.cadw.wales.gov.uk. **Oceanarium** is the biggest sea aquarium in west Wales. Open all year 1000–1800 during school holidays; closes at 1700 or 1600 at other times of year. Charge. Telephone (01437) 720453. **St David's Farm Park** is a working farm and home to rare breeds. Café and craft shop. Picnic area and adventure playground. Open April to October, daily 1000–1700. Charge. Telephone (01437) 721601. Bookings for boat trips to Ramsey Island (see C) and bicycle hire can be made at **Thousand Islands Expeditions** in St David's, telephone (01437) 721686; www.ramseyisland.co.uk. **Voyages of Discovery** run boat trips around the island. Telephone (01437) 721911. For more information on St Davids, contact the National Park Visitor Centre (see page 13) or visit www.stdavids.co.uk

B Porth Clais Harbour

A picturesque harbour within the Pembrokeshire Coast National Park. Restored limekilns show that lime was landed here to be spread on local fields. Contact St David's National Park Visitor Centre for more details.

C Ramsey Island

Ramsey Island is a bird reserve administered by the RSPB. Visitor numbers are limited per day and boat trips can be booked through Thousand Island Expeditions (see A). Voyages of Discovery (see A) run boat trips around the island, allowing visitors to view the birdlife and spot Atlantic grey seals from the sea. Ramsey Island reserve open Easter to October, daily except Tuesday. Boats cross, weather permitting, from the lifeboat station at St Justinians at 1000 and 1300, returning at 1315 and 1600.

Food and drink

Plenty of choice in St David's during summer. Outside the holiday season some of the cafés will be closed and cyclists should carry food and drink to sustain them during the ride.

Rhosygihwen Dairy Tearooms, near St David's
Soft drinks and snacks available.

Bishop's Palace

LLANWRTYD WELLS AND LLANGAMMARCH WELLS

Route information

Distance   22.5km (14 miles)

Grade   Moderate

Terrain   Well-surfaced, gently undulating minor roads and a stretch of A road in Llanwrtyd. There is one steep climb out of Llangammarch.

Time to allow   1–3 hours.

Getting there by car   Llanwrtyd Wells in on the A483, between Llandovery and Builth Wells. There are several long-term car parks – the most convenient for the start of the route (and free of charge) is behind the Nuedd Arms pub.

Getting there by train   There is a railway station at Llanwrtyd Wells. See page 13 for travel information.

An opportunity to cycle on quiet country roads with expansive views. From the small town of Llanwrtyd Wells, the route briefly heads east for excellent views of the Eppynt Mountains. On to follow the River Irfon to Llangammarch Wells. From here the route loops around to Garth, before continuing to Cefn Glancamddwr and back to Llanwrtyd Wells. Just by Cefn Glancamddwr is a long straight road of Roman origin. The route can be shortened by avoiding the loop to Garth, making a total distance of 14.5km (9 miles).

Places of interest along the route

Ⓐ Llanwrtyd Wells

This small spa town on the River Irfon is said to be the smallest town in Britain, with a population of approximately 650. The town is well-known for its off-road cycling and is known as the birthplace of mountain biking in the UK. The CTC have several waymarked routes here and there is much cycling activity. Also cycle shop and hire. Telephone the Tourist Information Centre for more details (see page 13).

Ⓑ Llangammarch Wells

Llangammarch Wells is one of the smallest spa villages and sits at the confluence of the Rivers Cammarch and Irfon. The mineral springs contain barium chloride, unique in Britain.

Food and drink

There is plenty of choice in Llanwrtyd Wells.

Nuedd Arms, Llanwrtyd Wells
Bar snacks and meals available.

Aberdulas Inn, near Llangammarch
A riverside pub serving bar meals.

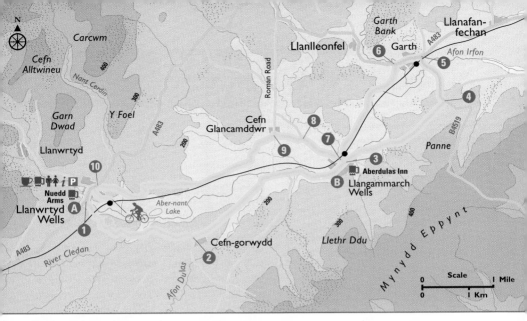

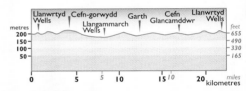

Route description

TL out of railway station and into Llanwrtyd Wells town centre. TL onto A483 SP, Llandovery.

From public car park at rear of Nuedd Inn retrace to front of Nuedd Inn and TR onto A483 SP Llandovery.

1 TL, SP Llangammarch Wells. Continue along this road into Cefn-gorwydd.

2 TL at XR, SP Llangammarch Wells, and continue into Llangammarch Wells.

3 To take the short cut, bypassing Garth, TL at TJ, SP Cefn (7km/4.5 miles). Rejoin the main route at direction 7, where TL, no SP.

Otherwise, to continue route, TR, SP Upper Chapel, and continue along this road.

4 TL at XR onto B4519, SP Garth, and continue into village.

5 TL at XR onto A483, SP Beulah.

6 TL, SP Llangammarch Wells.

7 Descend under railway bridge and TR at TJ, no SP (14.5km/9 miles). Climb out of Llangammarch Wells.

8 TL, SP Llanwrtyd Wells. Continue into Cefn Glancamddwr.

9 TL, SP Llanwrtyd Wells.

10 TL at TJ onto A483 and continue into Llanwrtyd Wells to finish the ride.

22.5km (14 miles)

THE GOWER PENINSULA – GOWERTON AND LLANRHIDIAN

Route information

 Distance   27km (17 miles)

Grade   Easy

Terrain   Mostly quiet country lanes and a stretch of B road. There are some sharp descents and the road surfaces are poor in places – young children should to be closely supervised.

Time to allow   2–4 hours.

Getting there by car   Gowerton is 8km (5 miles) north west of Swansea. From the M4 take the A483 (junction 47). Then take the A484 and the B4296 to Gowerton. From Swansea take the A483 and the B4295. Park in Sterry Road car park (on the B4295, just after Ty Gwyn Mawr pub).

Getting there by train   Gowerton has a railway station. See page 13 for travel information.

A short circuit around the north side of the Gower Peninsula, a designated Area of Outstanding Natural Beauty and inhabited by man for over 30,000 years. A place of deserted beaches, pretty villages and quiet country roads. From the small town of Gowerton the route heads west towards the coast and then down to Llanrhidian. From here you can extend the route to take in Arthur's Stone and an ancient burial chamber, before heading back to Gowerton.

Places of interest along the route

A Llanrhidian

Llanrhidian sits on a steep slope overlooking Lhanrhidian Sands, a large area of mud and sand flats on the south side of the River Loughor estuary (National Trust property). The area provides grazing for sheep and ponies and is a source of food for many different birds, including starlings, curlew, snip and duck. Visitors should keep to the paths and be aware of incoming tides. **Llanrhidian Church** originally dates from the 13th century and was renovated during the 19th century. It contains strikingly carved altar and ceiling bosses, and a fragment from a 9th-century Viking sarcophagus. There is a natural spring, beside a small cave near the west wall of the churchyard.

B Gower Studio, near Llanrhidian

The studio exhibits over 40 original water colours and oil paintings, many of local scenes. Telephone (01792) 391196 to confirm opening times.

C Arthur's Stone, Cefn Bryn

Cefn Bryn is a sandstone ridge, the second highest point on the Gower Peninsula. It was a focal point for prehistoric man and there are over sixty burial mounds in the area. The most impressive prehistoric remain is Arthur's Stone, which dates from around 2500BC. Free access at all reasonable times.

For more information on the Gower Peninsula, contact Mumbles Tourist Information Centre (see page 13) or visit www.explore-gower. co.uk

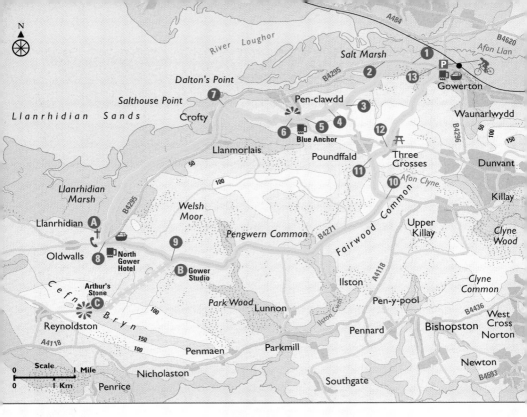

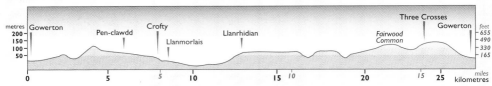

Route description

If starting from the railway station, leave the station and walk through Station Road to Sterry Road and the car park.

TR out of car park into Sterry Road. Pass Ty Gwyn Mawr pub on RHS and Welcome to Gower pub on LHS.

1 TL at junction, SP Gower/Llanrhidian B4295.

2 TL at TJ, SP Wern/Three Crosses.

3 TR at TJ (after National Speed Limit SP).
4km (2.5 miles)

4 LHF (scrap yard on LHS). CARE down steep hill with poor surface.

5 TR at TJ (Blue Anchor pub on LHS). Good views here. Continue SO at XR through estate.

6 TL at TJ by greenhouses.

Arthur's Stone

7 TL at TJ, SP Llanrhidian (8km/5 miles). TR into Pencaerfenni Lane. Continue along this road into Llanrhidian, with Llanrhidian Sands on RHS.

8 TL to visit Llanrhidian church.

Otherwise, to continue route, SO at XR (garage shop on LHS, North Gower Hotel on RHS).

12.5km (8 miles)

9 Arrive Gower Studios on RHS. To visit Cefn Bryn and Arthur's Stone (extra 4.5km/ 3 miles) TR.

Otherwise, SO and continue along this road.

10 TL into Tirmynydd Road, SP Three Crosses. *22.5km (14 miles)*

11 TR into Chapel Road, SP Three Crosses/ Golf Club.

12 SO at XR, SP Golf Club (picnic area here). Continue along this road into Gowerton.

13 TR at XR into Sterry Road and walk along one-way road back to car park and the end of the ride. *27km (17 miles)*

Food and drink

There are two pubs and a convenience store in Gowerton. Llanrhidian also has a convenience store.

North Gower Hotel, Llanrhidian
Bar meals available.

MANORBIER, CAREW AND ST FLORENCE

Route information

Distance 29km (18 miles)

Grade Moderate

Terrain Well-surfaced, undulating country lanes with short, sharp climbs, wonderful descents and plenty of easy cycling. The roads are generally quiet but Carew can be busy during the summer.

Time to allow 3–4 hours.

Getting there by car Manorbier is 6.5km (4 miles) south west of Tenby on the A3139 and B4585. Head through Manorbier and park at the beach car park, opposite Manorbier Castle.

Getting there by train Manorbier Newton has a station. Most trains stopping at the station carry bicycles but cyclists should book their travel in advance. See page 13 for travel information.

This route takes you around some of the special places of Pembrokeshire, missed by many car-borne visitors. The ride starts from Manorbier Castle, which dominates the town and offers spectacular views across to St Govan's Head, the most southerly point in Pembrokeshire. Heading west you climb beside the beach and turn inland to the picturesque

village of Manorbier Newton (look out for the Victorian postbox). The route climbs up to the Ridgeway for splendid views back to Manorbier Bay and north to the Prescelly Mountains before descending to Carew, a perfect lunch stop. From Carew the route follows the Cresswell River to Cresswell. The route now climbs to the idyllic village of St Florence before crossing the Ridgeway once more to return to Manorbier. The route follows sections of the National Cycle Network (Celtic Trail/NCR 4).

Places of interest along the route

Ⓐ Manorbier Castle

Manorbier Castle overlooks the beach and bay and was built during the 12th century by the medieval chronicler of Welsh history, Geraldus Cambrenis. Visitors can see the well-preserved castle remains and the beautiful gardens. Open Easter to end September, daily 1030–1730. Charge. Telephone (01834) 871394.

Ⓑ Carew

A picturesque village on the easterly tip of the Cleddau Estuary. **Carew Castle** is situated on the shore of a mill pond. The castle was built as a Norman stronghold and then converted to a manor house, before being ruined during the civil war in the 17th century. Administered by Pembrokeshire Coast National Park Authority. Good picnic spot. **Carew Tidal Mill** is a 19th-century corn mill powered by the

Manorbier Castle

tide. Castle and mill open Easter to October, daily 1000–1700. Charge. Telephone (01646) 651782.

ⓒ St Florence
A pretty village (previous winner of the Village in Bloom award) passed through towards the end of the ride and well-known for its fine Flemish chimneys. Just to the north of the village is Manor House Wildlife and Leisure Park, with a large collection of animals, birds, fish and reptiles, gardens and children's rides. Tearoom and bar. Open Easter to September, daily 1000–1800. Telephone (01646) 651201.

Food and drink

Manorbier has a tearoom, pub and village shop, and there are pubs and a shop in St Florence. Refreshment are also available at Manor House Wildlife and Leisure Park.

🍺 **Carew Inn, Carew**
Good home-cooked meals.

🍺 **Cresselly Arms, Cresswell**
Popular pub serving food.

☕ **Bramleys Tearoom, St Florence**
A convenient stop on the return journey. This tearoom has won prizes for its cakes.

Route description

If starting from Manorbier Newton Station, TR off platform, across railway lines and take first TR down lane, SP Manorbier Newton. Ignore TL and join route at direction 2, where SO at XR.

From Manorbier, TL out of car park and climb road overlooking beach (views to St Govan's Head). SO at XR up slight hill. Keep SO to arrive at A4139 in Jameston.

1 TR at TJ (with CARE, busy road) and take next TL, opposite Swan Lake Inn. Continue on this road, ignoring minor roads on LHS/RHS.

2 TL at XR before crossing railway lines, no SP (3km/2 miles). Continue into Manorbier Newton.

3 TR opposite Victorian postbox, over railway lines and climb hill, following RHF to Ridgeway.

4 TL at TJ onto Ridgeway and join Celtic Trail (views south to Manorbier, north to Prescelly Mountains). Continue to next junction.

5 TR, SP Milton, leaving Celtic Trail. Continue with CARE down hill to TJ with busy A477.

6 TR onto A477 with CARE (8km/5 miles). Take second TL, SP Carew/A4075. Cycle down hill, past Carew Inn and castle and over bridge.

7 TL, SP West Williamston. Stay on this road into West Williamston, ignoring all junctions to right.

8 Take LHF to Cresswell Quay. Continue on this road.

9 TL at TJ, down hill to Cresswell Quay.

10 TR, past telephone box and up hill to TJ at Cresselly.

11 TR and continue to A4075 XR, where SO, SP Jeffreyston. *16km (10 miles)*

12 TR then SO at XR and continue on this road.

13 TR at TJ and continue to junction with A477.

14 TR then immediately TL (CARE), SP St Florence. Continue to XR with B4318.

15 SO at XR and down hill into St Florence, passing Manor House Wildlife and Leisure Park on LHS, then Bramleys Tearoom on RHS.

16 Follow one-way system through village, past Sun Inn and Flemish Chimney pub. TL at TJ down hill, SP Manorbier. Pass pub and village shop and follow road as it climbs a 17% hill back up to Ridgeway.

17 SO at XR at top of hill, SP Manorbier (24km/15 miles). Then again, SO at XR, SP Manorbier. Cycle down through village, past shop, Castle Inn and Chives Tearooms. TL down hill, alongside castle, to return to the car park and the end of the ride. *29km (18 miles)*

If returning to the Manorbier Newton Station follow route directions 1 and then 2, where TR at XR and retrace to station.

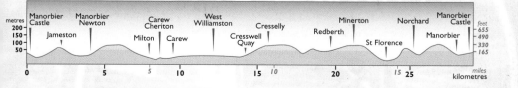

LLANTWIT MAJOR AND EWENNY

Route information

Distance 33.5km (21 miles)

Grade Easy

Terrain Well-surfaced minor and B roads, mainly flat except for one steep hill out of Ewenny. The roads are generally quiet outside the holiday season but the B4524 between Ogmore-by-Sea and Ewenny can be busy on Sundays in summer and on Bank Holiday Mondays.

Time to allow 2–4 hours.

Getting there by car Llantwit Major is 6.5km (4 miles) south of Cowbridge on the B4270 and B4265. There is a free car park near the town centre.

Getting there by train The nearest station is at Bridgend, 4.5km (3 miles) from Ewenny. See page 13 for travel information.

A tour around the south west of the Vale of Glamorgan. From the town of Llantwit Major the route heads west and north to St Donat's and St Brides Major before turning and following the coast to Ogmore-by-Sea. On alongside the Ogmore River to Ewenny, before turning back to Llantwit Major. The route can be reduced, bypassing Ogmore-by-Sea, reducing the total distance to 29km (18 miles).

Route description

If starting from Bridgend railway station, follow B4365 to Ewenny and join route at direction 5, where TL, SP Corntown.

TR out of car park in Llantwit Major. TL at mini roundabout into Station Road. Then TL into High Street (becomes Commercial Street). Continue, ignoring first TR.

1 To visit Beach Café, TL.

Otherwise, to continue route, TR into The Strand. Continue on this road through St Donat's and Marcross (access to Nash Point), and on through Monknash to junction with B4265.

2 TL at TJ onto B4265, SP Bridgend.

3 To take short cut, bear right to stay on B4265 into Ewenny and rejoin route at direction 4 where TR.

Otherwise, to continue route, TL onto B4524, SP Southerndown/Ogmore (9.5km/6 miles). Follow this road through Southerndown, passing access to Glamorgan Heritage Coast Centre (100m behind beach car park), and continue through Ogmore-by-Sea and along River Ogmore.

4 TL at TJ onto B4265, SP Bridgend.

5 To visit Ewenny Priory, TL.

Otherwise, to continue route, almost immediately TR, SP Corntown.

6 TR (on brow of hill), SP Colwinston/ Llandow (20km/12.5 miles). Continue, ignoring first TL (Stoney Lane).

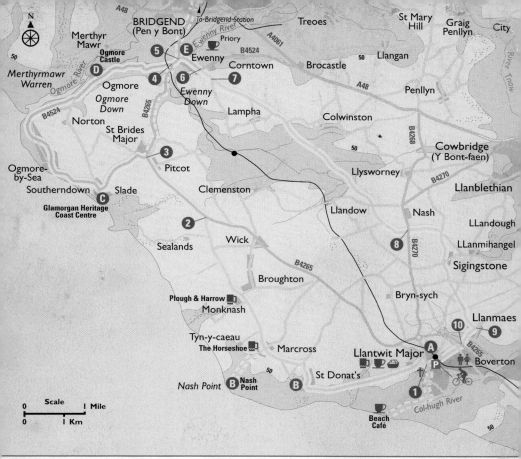

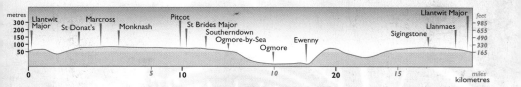

7   TL at at three-way junction, SP Lampha/Colwinston, and continue along this road to XR with B4270.

8   SO at XR, no SP (27km/17 miles). Continue through Sigingstone into Llanmaes.

9   TR at TJ, SP Llantwit Major.

10   SO at traffic lights with B4265. Continue under railway bridge, TL at mini roundabout and return to car park on LHS to finish the ride.

33.5km (21 miles)

Places of interest along the route

A Llantwit Major

A small town of narrow streets and stone buildings, and the site of a monastery and school of divinity built by St Illtud, a 6th-century Breton saint. **St Illtud's Church** was built on the site of the monastery and contains a fine collection of Celtic crosses. For more information contact Bridgend Tourist Information Centre (see page 13).

B St Donat's and Nash Point

Thirteenth-century **St Donat's Castle** retains many original features. Today it is home to Atlantic College, the world's first international sixth form college. Guided tours of the castle are available in summer. Telephone (01446) 799100 for details. The headland at Nash Point has barely visible remains of a long cairn and an Iron Age fort, probably built to defend the coast from raiders around 700 BC. There are two lighthouses on **Nash Point.** They were built following the sinking of the *Frolic* in 1832 with the loss of 40 lives. The lighthouse towers are positioned so that they can be aligned by ships sailing up the channel. There is also a signed nature trail on the point.

C Glamorgan Heritage Coast Centre, Southerndown

The Heritage Coast was designated such in the early 1970s to protect 22.5km (14 miles) of stunning coastline between Porthcawl and Gileston. The centre describes the coast and its cliffs, sand dunes and beaches. Free admission. Telephone (01656) 880157 to confirm opening times.

D Ogmore Castle, Merthyr Mawr

The ruins of a castle built in the 12th and 13th centuries to defend the ford on the Ogmore River. Visitors can cross to the castle via stepping stones but care should be taken as the river levels can charge rapidly. Cadw property. Free access at all reasonable times. Telephone (01222) 500261; www.cadw.wales.gov.uk

E Ewenny

The ruins of **Ewenny Priory**, founded in 1141, sit on the banks of the River Ewenny. Cadw property. Free access at all reasonable times. Telephone (01222) 500261; www.cadw.wales.gov.uk. The village church, founded at the same time as the priory, contains Norman inscriptions. **Ewenny Craft Centre** is home to Ewenny Pottery, founded in 1815 and still owned by the Jenkins family. Also pine shop and Welsh craft shop. Tearoom. Open all year, Monday–Saturday 1000–1700. Admission free. Telephone (01656) 653020.

Food and drink

Plenty of choice in Llantwit Major and refreshments are available at Ewenny Craft Centre.

Beach Café, Llantwit Major
Open daily in summer for snacks and meals.

The Horseshoe, Marcross
Bar meals served.

Plough and Harrow, Monknash
Offers real ale and meals.

FISHGUARD, STRUMBLE HEAD AND CASTLE MORRIS

Route information

Distance   33.5km (21 miles)

Grade   Moderate

Terrain   Mostly quiet lanes, except for the route out of and back into Fishguard.

Time to allow   3–5 hours.

Getting there by car   Fishguard is approximately 21km (13 miles) north of Haverfordwest on the A40 and A487. There is plenty of parking in the town. The most convenient is by the railway station (signposted).

Getting there by train   There is a railway station at Fishguard, but the service is infrequent. See page 13 for travel information.

From Fishguard the route heads west to Strumble Head, passing the site of prehistoric burial mounds along the way. From Strumble Head the route turns south to the village of Castle Morris, before heading back to Fishguard.

Places of interest along the route

Ⓐ Fishguard

The town has a picturesque old harbour and quayside at the south end of Fishguard Bay.

The harbour was used as a location during filming of *Under Milk Wood* in the 1970s. The new harbour is at Goodwick, from where ferries leave for Ireland. The last invasion of Britain took place near to Fishguard in 1779 when a small French force landed at Carregwastad Point – the French surrendered just two days later to local resistance. The **Fishguard Tapestry**, St Mary's Church Hall, Main Street, commemorates this event. Open April to October, Monday–Saturday 1000–1700, Sunday 1400–1700. **Ocean Lab**, Seafront, Goodwick, is a simulated submarine adventure featuring prehistoric sea creatures (created by the Jim Henderson Company, the creators of the Muppets). Also coffee and craft shop, cyber café and tearoom. Charge. Open Easter to October, daily 1000–1800. Charge. Telephone (01348) 874737.

Ⓑ Strumble Head

A lighthouse stands on the headland. There are superb views from here and, sometimes, the chance to see seals.

Ⓒ Llangloffan Farmhouse Cheese, Llangloffan

Award-winning farmhouse cheese-makers, using traditional equipment and methods. Demonstrations, farm shop and tearoom. Open 0900–1730 April and October, Monday–Friday; May–September, Monday–Saturday; demonstrations held 1000–1245. Charge. Telephone (01348) 891241; www.welshcheese.co.uk

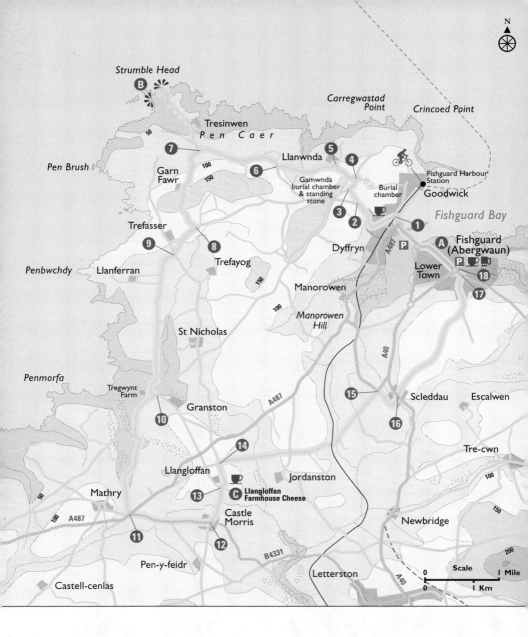

N

Strumble Head
B

Carregwastad Point

Crincoed Point

Tresinwen
Pen Caer

Llanwnda
5 **4**

Fishguard Harbour Station

Pen Brush

Garn Fawr

100

150

7

6

Gamwnda burial chamber & standing stone

Burial chamber

Goodwick

3

2

Fishguard Bay

Trefasser

8

Dyffryn

1

A Fishguard (Abergwaun)

9

Trefayog

150

Lower Town

18

Penbwchdy

Llanferran

Manorowen

17

100

Manorowen Hill

St Nicholas

Penmorfa

Tregwynt Farm

Granston

A487

15 Scleddau Escalwen

10

A40

16

Tre-cwn

14

Llangloffan

Jordanston

100

13

C Llangloffan Farmhouse Cheese

Mathry

150

Castle Morris

Newbridge

50

100 A487

11

12

200

Pen-y-feidr

B4331

Scale

1 Mile

Castell-cenlas

Letterston

A40

1 Km

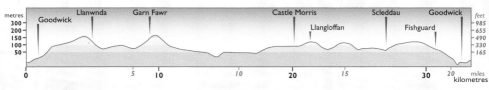

metres									feet
300	Goodwick	Llanwnda	Garn Fawr		Castle Morris		Scleddau	Goodwick	985
200						Llangloffan		Fishguard	655
150									490
100									330
50									165

0   5   10   10   20   15   30   20   miles
kilometres

Route description

Leave Fishguard Harbour railway station and car park following SP Exit. Continue to roundabout (junction of A40 and A487) and take third exit, SP Goodwick. Continue into Goodwick.

1 TL at TJ, SP Strumble Head/Llanwnda, and climb.

2 SO, SP Llanwnda.

3 TR at TJ, SP Llanwnda.

4 To visit burial chamber, TR.

Otherwise, to continue route, TL at XR, no SP. Continue into Llanwnda.

5 Bear L in Llanwnda (3km/2 miles), taking unsurfaced road, SP Unsuitable For Motors. Follow this road for 1km (0.6 mile), passing Gamwnda burial chamber and standing stone on LHS.

6 TR at TJ, joining surfaced road.

7 To visit Strumble Head, TR SP Strumble Head.   *8km (5 miles)*

Otherwise, continue on this road for climb and descent through Garn Fawr.

8 TR at TJ, SP Pwllderi/St Nicholas.

9 SO at XR, SP Tregwynt Woollen Mill. Descend (CARE – sharp bend and narrow lane). Climb to Tregwynt Farm.

10 TR at XR (16km/10 miles). Continue to five-way junction with A487.

11 Cross A487 (CARE) onto B4331, SP Letterston. Follow this road into Castle Morris.

12 TL at XR, SP Llangloffan. Continue into Llangloffan.

13 Bear R in Llangloffan. Continue out of village, passing Llangloffan Farm.

14 TR at XR, no SP (22.5km/14 miles). Continue to junction with A4219, passing under railway.

15 TR (NOT onto A4219), SP Scleddau. Continue through village.

16 SO at XR over A40 (CARE), no SP (26.5km/16.5 miles). Continue towards Fishguard.

17 SO at XR, onto B4313.

18 TL at TJ onto A487. At roundabout in town centre take second exit, SP Goodwick. At next roundabout again take second exit, SP Goodwick. Descend to seafront and take third exit at roundabout to return to station and the end of the ride.   *33.5km (21 miles)*

Food and drink

There are several cafés and pubs in Fishguard and refreshments are available at Ocean Lab and Llangloffan Farmhouse Cheese. Out of the tourist season it is difficult to get lunchtime meals in the countryside. Cyclists should carry food and drink to sustain them during the ride.

CALDICOT AND WENTWOOD

Route information

Distance 35.5km (22 miles)

Grade Moderate

Terrain Quiet, winding lanes and a few sections of untarred road. There is one long climb to Wentwood

Time to allow 3–4 hours.

Getting there by car The route starts from the Severn Tunnel Junction, where there is parking (access via M4, junction 23). Caldicot, close to the start, is 8km (5 miles) south west of Chepstow on the B4245, close to the M4, junction 23. There is parking in town.

Getting there by train Severn Tunnel Junction Station is served by trains from Cardiff, Birmingham and Bristol. The route passes Caldicot Station. Note that reservations are required on some trains and cyclists should book in advance. See page 13 for travel information.

A ride of contrasts, from the the low-lying Caldicot Levels at the mouth of the River Severn, to the hilltops of Wentwood Forest, climbing from near sea level to over 300m (984 feet). From the Severn Tunnel Junction, near Caldicot, the route runs west to Magor before climbing to Wentwood. From here you circuit to Shirenewton before descending to Caldicot. The route follows sections of the National Cycle Network (NCR 4 and 42).

Places of interest along the route

Ⓐ Severn Tunnel Junction, near Caldicot

The tunnel, 6.5km (4 miles) long beneath the River Severn, was opened in 1886 and was built primarily to transport coal from the coalfields of south Wales to England. An important railway centre developed here, but the once extensive engine sheds and sidings have all gone.

Ⓑ Wentwood Forest

An ancient forest with the remains of the original oak and beech and the more recently planted spruce and larch. More than 130 species of bird have been recorded in the area, including buzzards, kestrels and owls. Waymarked routes, picnic and barbeque areas. Forestry Commission property. Castell Troggy, near Llantrisant, is all that remains of a hunting lodge built in the early 14th century. Free access at all reasonable times. For more information, telephone (01970) 612367; www.forestry.gov.uk

Ⓒ Caerwent

In Roman times Caerwent (*Venta Silurum*) was the largest town in south Wales. Today visitors can see the remains of the defensive walls and a temple, built circa 330 AD. A display board outside Caerwent Church provides a key to the sites. Cadw property. Free access at all reasonable times. Telephone (02920) 500200; www.cadw.wales.gov.uk

D Caldicot Castle and Country Park, Caldicot

A Norman castle built in the late 14th century. Parts of the castle were restored as family home during the 18th century and today visitors can explore the medieval walls and towers, gardens and woodland. Tours, picnic and barbeque areas, shop and tearoom. Open March to October, Saturday 1030–1700, Sunday 1330–1700. Charge. Telephone (01291) 420241.

Food and drink

There are pubs, shops and cafés in Caldicot and Magor, and two pubs in Shirenewton. Refreshments are available at Caldicot Castle and Country Park. There are no villages on the central part of the route so provisions should be obtained before leaving Magor.

Groeswen Inn, near Parc-Seymour
Food available all day.

Coach & Horses, Caerwent
Open all day. Meals served.

Left: *Forestry*   Right: *Caerwent*

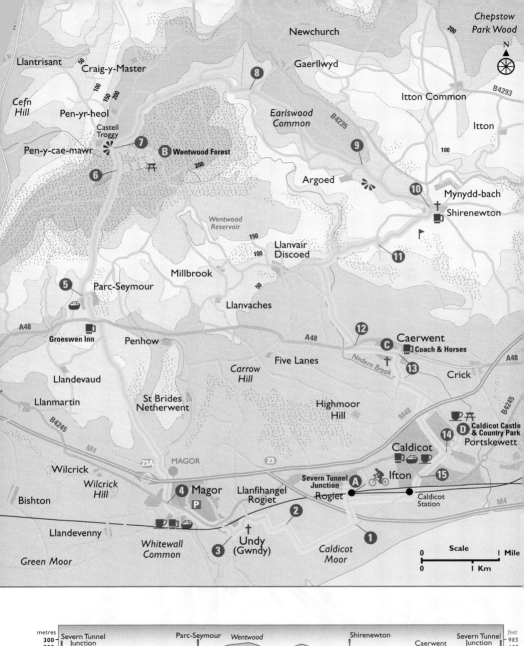

Newchurch

Chepstow
Park Wood

Gaerllwyd

N

Llantrisant

Craig-y-Master

8

Itton Common

B4293

Cefn
Hill

Pen-yr-heol

Earlswood
Common

B4235

Itton

Pen-y-cae-mawr

Castell
Troggy

7

B Wentwood Forest

9

100

Mynydd-bach

Shirenewton

6

200

Argoed

10

Wentwood
Reservoir

150

Llanvair
Discoed

100

11

5

Parc-Seymour

Millbrook

50

A48

Groeswen Inn

Penhow

Llanvaches

A48

12

Caerwent

C Coach & Horses

A48

Llandevaud

Carrow
Hill

Five Lanes

Nedern Brook

13

Crick

B4245

Llanmartin

St Brides
Netherwent

Highmoor
Hill

M48

Caldicot Castle
& Country Park

D

Portskewett

B4245

B4245

M4

Wilcrick

MAGOR

Caldicot

14

Ifton

15

Bishton

Wilcrick
Hill

23A

23

Severn Tunnel
Junction

A

Caldicot
Station

M4

Llandevenny

Whitewall
Common

4 Magor
P

Llanfihangel
Rogiet

Rogiet

2

1

Green Moor

3

Undy
(Gwndy)

Caldicot
Moor

Scale

0   1 Mile

0   1 Km

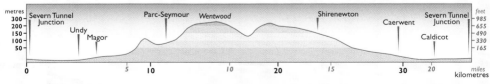

metres
300
200
150
100
50

Severn Tunnel
Junction

Undy

Magor

Parc-Seymour

Wentwood

Shirenewton

Caerwent

Severn Tunnel
Junction

Caldicot

feet
985
655
490
330
165

0   5   10   15   20   miles
         10   20   30   kilometres

Route description

From Caldicot Station TR into private road (NCR 4). Continue along this narrow tarred road between M4 and railway to TJ where TL. Continue SO over M4 and start route at direction 1.

From Severn Tunnel Junction Station, TR out of station and TL to cross railway west of station, keeping SO over M4.

1 Arrive TJ where tarmac ends. TR and continue along stone-surfaced lane. At end of long straight, TR at TJ to head north. This section of the route, as far as Undy XR, is NCR 4 (stickers at junctions).

2 TL at TJ (4km/2.5 miles). Road becomes tarred by houses. Continue for 300m to TL and TL again into Undy village. Pass church and Well Garage.

3 TR at XR and over railway. TL at XR onto B4245. Continue along B4245 into Magor (village centre/shops/pubs to left).

4 TR, SP St Brides Netherwent (7km/4.5 miles). Pass under M4, then LHF into Bowdens Lane, no SP. SO to A48 by Groeswen Inn. TL then immediately TR towards Parc-Seymour. Continue uphill through village (post office/shop on LHS), bearing L. Continue to end of houses.

5 RHF into narrow lane (11km/7 miles). Continue uphill into Wentwood – a long climb, steep in places.

6 To avoid steep descent and to visit Wentwood, at summit of hill TR onto good track along ridge. Pass picnic site and continue route at direction 7, where TR, SP Shirenewton.

Otherwise, continue SO (CARE on descent) to foot of hill.

7 SO at staggered XR, SP Shirenewton (NCR 4). Pass Castell Troggy and continue as road drops down valley, keeping SO to steep rise beyond bridge.

8 TR at XR (18.5km/11.5 miles). Then SO, initially uphill then long gradual descent.

9 TR and continue towards Shirenewton.

10 TR at XR, skirting church. Then TR and skirt golf course.

11 TR then immediately TL (25km/15.5 miles). Continue and TL at bridge, then TL twice, SP Caerwent, and continue to junction with A48.

12 TR onto A48 (CARE) then immediately TL (or walk across) and follow old Roman road into Caerwent. Continue to east end of village, passing church.

13 TR at XR (29.5km/18.5 miles), following old Roman walls. TL at hillfoot for 400m, then TR (onto NCR 4). Continue uphill, under M48 and along stony lane parallel to motorway. After 200m this becomes residential road (Sandy Lane). Keep SO into Caldicot. There is a cycle track on LHS just after motorway (not a through route at time of printing).

14 To visit Caldicot Castle and Country Park, TL at roundabout.

Otherwise, to continue route, TR at roundabout into Jubilee Way (town centre precinct may be reached through car park on LHS). TR at end of Jubilee Way into Newport Road, passing cycle shop.

15 SO at traffic lights, passing under railway at Caldicot Station. On south side of railway, TR into private road (NCR 4). Keep on this narrow tarred road between M4 and railway to TJ, where TR to Severn Junction Tunnel Station and the end of the ride. ***35.5km (22 miles)***

THE TAFF TRAIL – RADYR TO MERTHYR TYDFIL

Route information

Distance 36km (22.5 miles)

Grade Moderate

Terrain Mainly tarred off-road, some sections of urban road and a couple of steep climbs.

Time to allow 3–5 hours.

Getting there by car Radyr is 6.5km (4 miles) north west of Cardiff on the B4262, close to the M4, junction 33, and the A4119. There is a car park at the railway station. Alternatively the route may be started from Castell Coch, 7.5km (5 miles) north west of Cardiff, close to the M4, junction 32, on the A4054. The car park opens and closes in conjunction with the castle.

Getting there by train Radyr Station is served by trains from Cardiff (some peak hour restrictions on travelling with bicycles). The route is paralleled by the Cardiff–Merthyr railway line and there are a number of stations from which you can return. It is best to check times before setting off. There are fewer trains north of Pontypridd, particularly on Sundays. See page 13 for travel information.

The Taff Trail is an 88.5km (55 mile) long trail of mainly off-road cycle track and footpath from Cardiff, up through the Taff Valley, to Brecon.

Our route is one-way, following the Taff Trail between Radyr and Merthyr Tydfil. The route can be shortened by finishing at Pontypridd (making the total distance 16km/10 miles). Return to the start of the route by train, or, turn around and retrace the route on your bicycle. Please remember to slow down when approaching walkers and horse riders, and ensure they are aware of you. NB: the Taff Trail is well signposted but future alterations to the route may result in slight variations to that described here.

There is plenty to see along the route and only a brief selection is described here. For more information and a detailed guide contact Cardiff Tourist Information Centre (see page 13) or the Taff Trail Project on (01685) 883880.

Places of interest along the route

A Castell Coch

A flamboyant reconstruction of a medieval fortress undertaken in the 1870s for the third Marquis of Bute, whose family had made a fortune from iron and coal. Cadw property. Open April to October, daily 0930–1830, November to March, Monday–Saturday 0930–1600, Sunday 1100–1600. Charge. Telephone (02920) 810101; www.cadw.wales.gov.uk

B Pontypridd

A busy market town at the junction of the Taff and Rhondda valleys. Famous for the soaring arched bridge, alongside the modern one in Bridge Street. The Historical and Cultural Centre also acts as a Tourist Information Centre. Open all year, times vary. Telephone (01443) 402077; www.pontypridd.org

C Penydarren Tramroad

This early railway ran from the ironworks at Merthyr to the Navigation Inn at Abercynon, where it joined the Glamorganshire Canal. The Taff Trail utilises the old track between Navigation and Pont y Gwaith. The tramroad became redundant when the Taff Vale Railway (which closely parallels the tramroad) was completed.

D Pont y Gwaith

A high-arched stone bridge in a pretty setting.

E Aberfan

Scene of the 1966 tragedy when a primary school was engulfed in slurry from the collapse of an ill-maintained spoil heap. The site of the school is now a Garden of Remembrance.

F Glamorganshire Canal

Much of the Taff Trail between Aberfan and Merthyr Tydfil follows the course of the Glamorganshire Canal, which fell into disuse over one hundred years ago. At one time the canal was so prosperous that tolls were abolished, but competition from the railways eventually led to a long and terminal decline.

G Merthyr Tydfil

The first wave of industrialisation in south Wales was the working of the ironstone deposits along the northern rim of the valleys. Merthyr Tydfil expanded to become the largest town in Wales in the early 1800s. As the iron industry waned and coal mining developed the town lost some of its pre-eminence and suffered severely during periods of economic depression. The original industries have now disappeared, although there is still some open-cast mining. The Taff Trail passes **Cyfarthfa Castle**, 2km (1 mile) north of the town centre. Built by the Crawshaw family of ironmasters, it now houses the town's museum and art gallery. Café. Open April to September, Monday–Friday 1000–1800; weekends and October to March, Monday–Saturday closes 1700. Telephone (01685) 723112; www.merthyr.gov.uk

Food and drink

There are numerous opportunities for refreshment along the Taff Trail. However, with a few exceptions, the pubs cater for local rather than tourist custom and do not offer a wide choice of food or drink. Cafés are scarce outside Pontypridd and Merthyr Tydfil, but all villages have a convenience store and usually a chip shop.

Route description

If starting from Castell Coch, join the route at direction 3.

Leave Radyr Station. Cross under railway south of station and over River Taff. TL to join Taff Trail northbound. Continue, pass under M4 and:

1   Join lane turning away from river, then TL, under A470 and enter Tongwynlais via Iron Bridge Road.

2   TL at TJ into Merthyr Road, pass cycle shop and continue into centre of village. TR into Mill Road. Continue uphill then LHF into driveway (steep hill) to Castell Coch.

3   From open area in front of castle (3km/2 miles) join Taff Trail as it doubles back up steep narrow path. At top of ascent, TL at TJ onto cart track through woods (well-surfaced at first, but care is required as it drops steeply to old bridge, from where route continues along old railway line). Continue to viewpoint.

4   At viewpoint (7km/4.5 miles) leave old railway for narrow lane alongside, which drops past house. Then follow Taff Trail as it leaves lane via gateway on L to join another cycle path (runs between Taff's Well and Caerphilly). Pass under road bridge and take LHF to climb to A468.

5 Cross A468 at pelican crossing and continue into housing estate. Take first TR to top of houses and join old railway. Continue along pleasant rural stretch of trail, eventually passing through housing estates where trail well-signed.

6 Old railway line abruptly ends (12.5km/ 8 miles). Keep on narrow path skirting cemetery, then follow narrow path (dismount) to Cemetery Road. Continue and TR at TJ onto A4054.

7 For Pontypridd and railway station, LHF into Ynysangharad Road through bollards (14.5km/9 miles). Arrive at roundabout below A470 and take second exit into Bridge Street (park on LHS). Cross River Taff and TL into Taff Street. This leads through town centre (part pedestrianised). Continue into High Street to reach railway station.

Otherwise, continue along Taff Trail (A4054) as far as SP Trallwyn.   ***15km (9.5 miles)***

8 TL under A470 (by SP Trallwyn) then TR at TJ by telephone box. Continue to end of road and LHF down to tarred lane which runs past fields and comes alongside river. Continue to barrier at end of track.   ***17.5km (11 miles)***

9 TR into lane, pass sports ground and school and TL to rise and cross over A470. TL at TJ onto A4054.

10 TL at traffic signals (19km/12 miles) and drop past Navigation pub as far as bridge (Abecynon Station is just over bridge). Just before bridge, TR into narrow lane and continue along riverside. Pass under viaduct, reach houses and keep SO at SP No Through Road to cross river.

11 To visit pubs and convenience store, TR at XR.

Otherwise, SO at XR. Continue as lane enters woods and recrosses river. Tarred section ends at barrier. Keep SO on uneven surface.

12 Arrive junction with steep lane (25km/15.5 miles). TL and cross river via steeply arched bridge (Pont y Gwaith). Continue up steep lane and take steps under A470. At top of steps TR into lane (above dual carriageway).

13 TR under A470 (steep descent) for 100m. TL onto track through Aberfan (village centre below on RHS, Merthyr Vale Station across valley). Continue SO as trail switches between disused canal and railway, into Troedyrhiw.

14 SO across road in Troedyrhiw (30.5km/19 miles). Railway station is across valley. Keep SO between house terraces and pass pub. Continue into Abercanaid.

15 For Pentrebach Station follow road past Sion chapel, below on R, and cross footbridge.

Otherwise, SO to stay on Taff Trail. Track is not always obvious but keep to disused canal and avoid parallel road. Pass under curious three-arch bridge then swing R to pass between Rhydycar Leisure Centre and River Taff.

16 Take footbridge over River Taff. To visit Cyfarthfa Castle, follow road to left.

Otherwise, to continue route into Merthyr Tydfil town centre, TL, cross road, TL at roundabout then LHF into part-pedestrianised area (High Street). TR into Masonic Street for railway station and the end of the ride. ***36km (22.5 miles)***

Return to Radyr on the train, or retrace route, following SP Taff Trail.

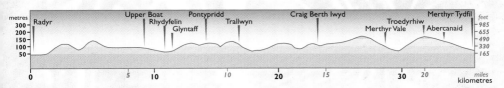

HAVERFORDWEST AND BROAD HAVEN

Route information

 Distance 41km (25.5 miles)

 Grade Moderate

Terrain Country lanes with some steep short climbs. The roads are generally quiet, except during July and August. There is one short stretch along an A road.

Time to allow 3–4 hours.

 Getting there by car Haverfordwest is 45km (28 miles) west of Carmarthen on the A40. There are several car parks in the town and parking at the railway station.

 Getting there by train The route starts from Haverfordwest Station, close to the town centre. See page 13 for travel information.

A route in south west Pembrokeshire, along minor roads that are lined with wild flowers from April onwards, and taking in part of the Pembrokeshire Coast National Park. From Haverfordwest the route circuits west to the coast and Nolton Haven. On along the coast to Broad Haven, and its fine beach. The route continues south and then turns east near Robestone Cross to head back to Haverfordwest.

Route description

Leave the railway station and follow SP for Town Centre. Take fourth exit at roundabout, SP Fishguard. At next roundabout, take first exit, SP St David's.

1 At roundabout, take fourth exit, SP Croesgoch B4330, and continue along this road.

2 LHF, SP Camrose (6.5km/4 miles). Continue into Camrose.

3 TL at XR and take first TR, SP Keeston. Continue into Keeston.

4 TR, then TL twice, SP St David's.
10.5km (6.5 miles)

5 TR, SP Unsuitable for Heavy Traffic. Continue, passing Pembrokeshire Motor Museum and cream teas.

6 TR at TJ onto A487 (CARE), SP St David's.

7 TL, SP Nolton Haven. Pass Hilton Court. Continue into Nolton Haven and pass Mariners Inn.

8 TL at TJ then TR, SP Druidston Haven (16km/10 miles). Climb, descend and climb again, passing Druidston House Hotel.

9 TR at TJ, SP Broad Haven. SO by church. Continue into Broad Haven.

10 TR at TJ onto B4341. TL into Walton Road.

11 TR, SP Rosepool.

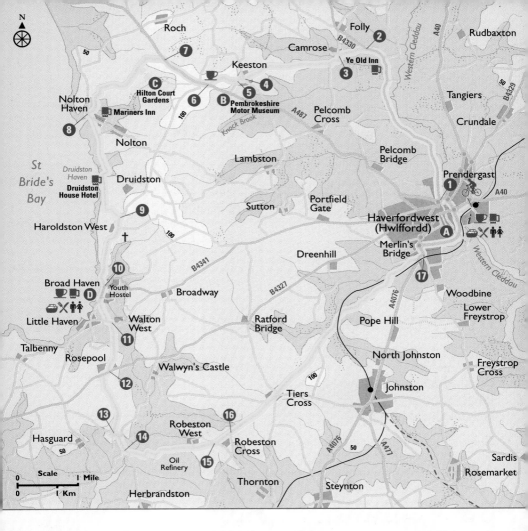

N

Roch

Folly ②
B4330

Camrose

Ye Old Inn ③

Keeston

Rudbaxton

Western Cleddau

A40

A40

50

⑦

④

⑤

Tangiers

B4329

50

C Hilton Court Gardens

⑥

B Pembrokeshire Motor Museum

A487

Pelcomb Cross

Crundale

Nolton Haven

Mariners Inn

⑧

Nolton

Knock Brook

Lambston

100

Pelcomb Bridge

Prendergast ①

A40

St Bride's Bay

Druidston Haven

Druidston House Hotel

Druidston

Sutton

Portfield Gate

Haverfordwest (Hwlffordd) Ⓐ

⑨

Haroldston West

Dreenhill

Merlin's Bridge

Western Cleddau

100

B4341

⑩

Broadway

B4327

Pope Hill

Woodbine

Lower Freystrop

Broad Haven D

Youth Hostel

A4076

Little Haven

Walton West

Ratford Bridge

North Johnston

Freystrop Cross

Talbenny

⑪

Rosepool

Walwyn's Castle

100

Johnston

Hasguard

⑫

Tiers Cross

A4076

⑬

⑯

Robeston West

A477

Sardis

50

⑭

Robeston Cross

50

Rosemarket

Oil Refinery

⑮

Thornton

Steynton

Scale
0   1 Mile
0   1 Km

Herbrandston

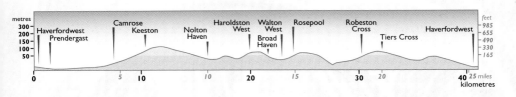

metres									feet
300	Camrose		Haroldston West	Walton West	Rosepool		Robeston Cross		985
200	Haverfordwest Keeston		Nolton	Broad				Haverfordwest	655
150	Prendergast		Haven	Haven			Tiers Cross		490
100									330
50									165

0   5   10   15   20   25 miles
0   10   20   30   40 kilometres

45

12 TR at TJ, SP Dale B4327 (24km/15 miles). Take first TL, SP Milford Haven, and continue along this minor road.

13 TL at TJ. Then take first TR, SP Milford Haven.

14 TL at TJ then TL, SP Robeston West. Pass Elf Oil Refinery on RHS.

15 SO at XR, SP Tiers Cross.

16 TL at TJ, SP Tiers Cross (31.5km/ 19.5 miles). Cycle through Tiers Cross, SP Haverfordwest, and continue to outskirts of town.

17 TL at TJ, SP Haverfordwest A4076. Take third exit at roundabout, onto Freemans Way (cycle path on LHS). Take third exit at round-about, SP Carmarthen. TR for station and the end of the ride.   ***41km (25.5 miles)***

Places of interest along the route

Ⓐ Haverfordwest

An ancient market town on the western Cleddau river. The town's castle is a ruin but adjacent is **Haverfordwest Town Museum**, which describes the history of the castle and town from the Middle Ages to the present day. Open Easter to October, Monday–Saturday 1000–1600. Charge. Telephone (01437) 763087. The old Augustian **Priory of SS Mary and Thomas the Martyr**, founded in 1207, can be seen from the cycle track along the Haverfordwest bypass.

Ⓑ Pembrokeshire Motor Museum, Keeston

Over 50 exhibits of veteran, vintage and classic motor vehicles and over 1500 model cars are on display. Open Easter to October, daily 1000–1700. Charge. Telephone (01437) 710950.

Ⓒ Hilton Court Gardens, near Nolton Haven

Hilton Court comprises over 3.6ha (9 acres) of gardens, woodland and lakes. Also craft work-shops, garden centre and tearoom. Open daily February to end May, 1030–1700; June to September, 1000–1800; October to December, 1030–1630. Charge. Telephone (01437) 710262.

Ⓓ Broad Haven

Broad Haven is part of the Pembrokeshire Coastal National Park. The award-winning beach is hemmed in at each end by cliffs and rocks. If visiting the rocks, be careful not to get cut off by the tide. The beach is popular with swimmers, and sail boarders and surfers when conditions are suitable. Good views across to St David's. For more information, contact the Tourist Information Centre at Haverfordwest (see page 13).

Food and drink

Plenty of choice in Haverfordwest and Broad Haven. Cream teas are available opposite Pembrokeshire Motor Museum.

Ⓓ **Ye Old Inn, Camrose**
Bar meals available.

Ⓓ **Mariners Inn, Nolton Haven**
Pub meals served.

Ⓓ **Druidston House Hotel, Druidston Haven**
Snacks and restaurant meals available, made from home grown produce.

Route information

Distance   45.5km (28.5 miles)

Grade   Moderate

Terrain   Mainly minor and B roads with a short stretch of A road. There are several short, steep climbs and one long one.

Time to allow   4–6 hours.

Getting there by car   Fishguard is approximately 21km (13 miles) north of Haverfordwest on the A40 and A487. There is plenty of parking in the town – this route starts from the Wallis Street car park, off the B4313 near the town centre.

Getting there by train   There is a railway station at Fishguard, but the service is infrequent. See page 13 for travel information.

A scenic ride in the Pembrokeshire Coast National Park, following a section of National Cycle Network (Celtic Cycle Trail). From Fishguard the route heads through Cwm Gwaun (Gwaun Valley), a Site of Special Scientific Interest with ancient woodland (and probably the best UK example of a geological phenomenon: a sub glacial melt water channel). The route turns south for a climb to Mynydd Du Commin, with excellent views over south Pembrokeshire. On to Tufton and the route turns north west back to Fishguard.

Route description

If starting from Fishguard Harbour railway station, leave station and car park following SP Exit. Continue to roundabout (junction of A40 and A487) and take first exit, SP Fishguard. Take first exit at next roundabout, SP Fishguard. Continue into town centre and take first exit at roundabout, SP Cardigan A487. Immediately TR, SP Maenclochog B4313. Continue SO into Wallis Street (do not follow SP Maenclochog).

TR out of Wallis Street car park and continue on this road in to Scleddau.

1   TL at XR onto A40, no SP.

2   TL, SP Trecwn/Llanychaer.

3   TL at TJ, SP Trecwn.

4   LHF (apparent SO), no SP. Do not go to Trecwn.   ***7km (4.5 miles)***

5   TR at TJ, SP Maenclochog/Cwm Gwaun B4313.

6   LHF, SP Cwm Gwaun (do not continue on B4313). Descend into Cwm Gwaun and continue along valley into Pontfaen.
                     14.5km (9 miles)

7   RHF, SP Penlan Uchaf Gardens 2 miles. Continue along this road (gardens on LHS), ignoring all turnings. Follow SP Maenclochog. Pass Cilgwyn Church on LHS and climb to junction.

8 RHF at junction, no SP.

20km (12.5 miles)

9 RHF by Trebwlch Farm, SP Maenclochog. Continue, passing standing stones on RHS.

10 TR at TJ onto B4329, SP Maenclochog. Climb to summit (404m/1325.5 feet) for excellent views. Descend with CARE – cattle grid and loose sheep!

11 To visit Old Post Office at Rosebush, TL at XR, SP Rosebush.

Otherwise, to continue route, SO at XR, SP Haverfordwest, and continue along B4329 into Tufton. *30.5km (19 miles)*

12 TR at XR, SP Puncheston, and continue into Castlebythe.

13 Next turn easy to miss – TL in Castlebythe, SP Puncheston (34.5km/21.5 miles). Continue into Puncheston, passing standing stones on RHS.

14 TR at TJ, SP Llanychaer. TL, SP Llanychaer, and continue to B4313, passing standing stones on LHS.

15 TL at TJ onto B4313, SP Fishguard.

40km (25 miles)

16 TR to stay on B4313 and follow this road back to Fishguard. TL into Wallis Street for the car park and the end of the ride.

45.5km (28.5 miles)

If you started from Fishguard Harbour Station continue along Wallis Street and retrace route back to station.

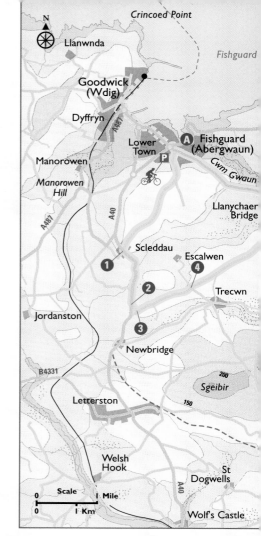

Places of interest along the route

🅐 Fishguard

The town has a picturesque old harbour and quayside, used as a location during filming of *Under Milk Wood* in the 1970s. See route 8 for more information.

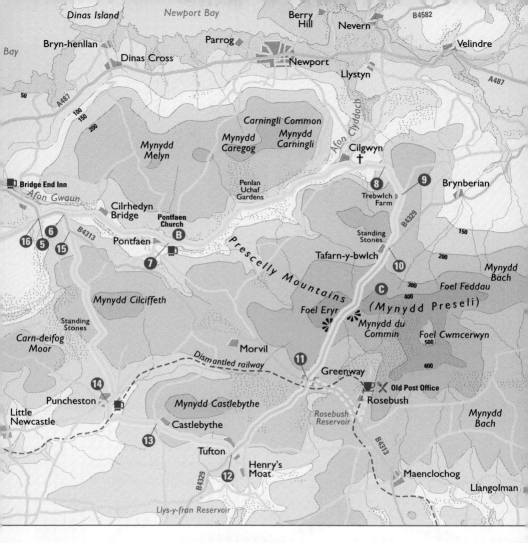

Dinas Island
Newport Bay
Berry Hill
Nevern
B4582

Bryn-henllan
Parrog
Velindre

Bay
Dinas Cross
Newport
Llystyn
A487

50
A487
Afon Clyddach
Cilgwyn
Carningli Common

100
Mynydd Caregog
Mynydd Carningli

150
Mynydd Melyn
Brynberian

200
Penlan Uchaf Gardens
8
9

Bridge End Inn
Trebwlch Farm
B4329
150

Afon Gwaun
Cilrhedyn Bridge
Pontfaen Church
Standing Stones
Tafarn-y-bwlch
200

B4313
Pontfaen
B
Mynydd Bach

16
6
7
Prescelly Mountains
10
300

5
15
C
400
Foel Feddau

Mynydd Cilciffeth
Foel Eryr
(Mynydd Preseli)

Standing Stones
Mynydd du Commin
Foel Cwmcerwyn

Carn-deifog Moor
Morvil
500

14
11
Dismantled railway
Greenway
400

Puncheston
Old Post Office

Little Newcastle
Mynydd Castlebythe
Rosebush Reservoir
Rosebush
Mynydd Bach

13
Castlebythe
B4313

Tufton
Henry's Moat
Maenclochog

B4329
12
Llangolman

Llys-y-fran Reservoir

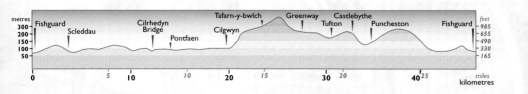

metres | Fishguard | Scleddau | Cilrhedyn Bridge | Pontfaen | Tafarn-y-bwlch | Cilgwyn | Greenway | Castlebythe | Tufton | Puncheston | Fishguard | feet
300 | | | | | | | | | | | | 985
200 | | | | | | | | | | | | 655
150 | | | | | | | | | | | | 490
100 | | | | | | | | | | | | 330
50 | | | | | | | | | | | | 165

0   5   10   10   20   15   30   20   40 25
kilometres   miles

Fishguard

Pontfaen Church, Pontfaen

This 9th-century church has two stones inscribed with crosses, dating from between the 7th and 9th centuries. Some residents of the remote hamlet of Pontfaen still celebrate the old Welsh new year (Hen Galan) on 13 January.

Mynydd Preseli

There are excellent views over south Pembrokeshire from the Mynydd Preseli, a ridge running east to west for 9.5km (6 miles) to the south and south east of Newport. This is mountain wilderness and there are a number of ancient standing stones in the area.

Food and drink

There are opportunities for refreshment in Fishguard. During the holiday season there are several pubs and a café open en route. However, out of season it can be difficult to find anywhere to eat or drink during the week and cyclists are advised to carry food and drink to sustain during them ride.

Bridge End Inn, Llanychaer
Bar meals served.

Old Post Office, Rosebush
Restaurant and tearoom.

HAY-ON-WYE, PAINSCASTLE AND GLADESTRY

Route information

Distance 46.5km (29 miles)

Grade Strenuous

Terrain Quiet lanes and B roads with a short stretch of A road.

Time to allow 3–5 hours.

Getting there by car Hay-on-Wye is 24km (15 miles) north east of Brecon on the B4350 (toll bridge) and B4348. There is a car park in the town, by the Tourist Information Centre.

Getting there by train There is no practical railway access to this route.

A route on the eastern edge of the Brecon Beacons National Park. From Hay-on-Wye the route heads north west over the Begwyns (National Trust) to Painscastle. On through Newchurch and Colva to Gladestry. Here the route turns south for the return to Hay-on-Wye. A shorter option can be followed, bypassing Gladestry (total distance 35.5km/22 miles, moderate). Superb views and picnic spots. The route follows a short section of National Cycle Network (NCR 25).

Places of interest along the route

A Hay-on-Wye
A market town situated on the River Wye, famous for its second-hand and antiquarian bookshops, and known as the Town of Books. Contact the Tourist Information Centre for more information (see page 13); www.hay-on-wye.co.uk

B Tawny Owl Animal Park, Wern Newydd
A family-run farm park. Lots of animals, crafts and gifts, woodland walks and excellent views. Open January to March, Friday and Saturday 1030–1600; April to September, daily except Wednesday 1000–1730; October to December, daily except Wednesday 1030–1600. Charge. Telephone (01497) 851399.

Food and drink

Plenty of choice in Hay-on-Wye and a shop at Clyro. There is no opportunity for refreshment between Clyro and Gladestry. Cyclists should carry food and drink to sustain them on this strenuous ride.

Royal Oak, Gladestry
Bar meals available.

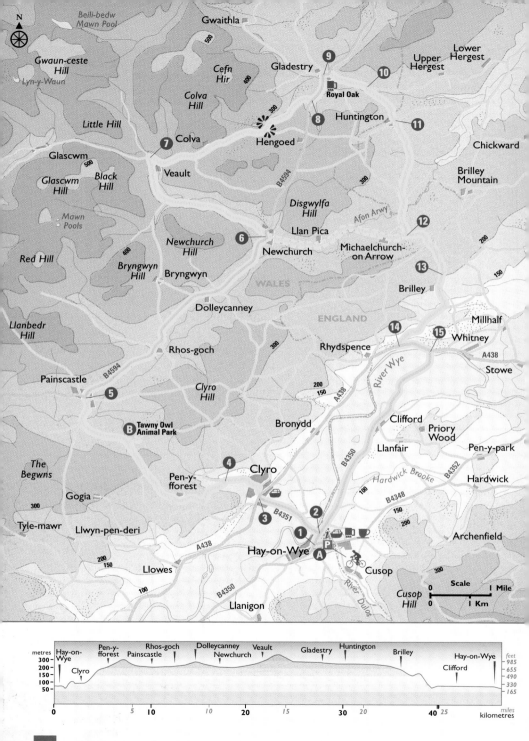

N

Beili-bedw
Mawn Pool

Gwaithla

Gwaun-ceste
Hill

Lyn-y-Waun

Cefn
Hir

Gladestry

⑨

Upper
Hergest

Lower
Hergest

⑩

Royal Oak

Colva
Hill

300

500

400

Little Hill

Hengoed

⑧

Huntington

⑪

Chickward

Colva

⑦

Brilley
Mountain

Glascwm

500

Veault

B4594

720

Disgwylfa
Hill

Afon Arrw

⑫

200

Glascwm
Hill

Black
Hill

Llan Pica

Michaelchurch-
on Arrow

⑬

150

Red Hill

400

Newchurch
Hill

⑥

Newchurch

Brilley

Mawn
Pools

Bryngwyn
Hill

Bryngwyn

WALES

ENGLAND

Millhalf

Llanbedr
Hill

Dolleycanney

300

Rhydspence

⑭

⑮

Whitney

A438

Rhos-goch

Painscastle

B4594

400

⑤

Clyro
Hill

300

200
150

A438

River Wye

Stowe

Clifford

Priory
Wood

Pen-y-park

Tawny Owl
Animal Park

Ⓑ

B4350

Llanfair

Hardwick

The
Begwns

④

Clyro

Hardwick Brooke

B4352

Pen-y-
fforest

③

B4451

②

100

B4348

Gogia

300

Llwyn-pen-deri

Tyle-mawr

①

150
200

Archenfield

A438

Hay-on-Wye

Ⓐ
P

200
150

Llowes

Cusop

100

Llanigon

B4350

River Dulos

Cusop
Hill

300

Scale

0   1 Mile

0   1 Km

metres
300
200
150
100
50

Hay-on-
Wye

Clyro

Pen-y-
fforest

Painscastle

Rhos-goch

Dolleycanney
Newchurch

Veault

Gladestry

Huntington

Brilley

Clifford

Hay-on-
Wye

feet
985
655
490
330
165

0   5   10   10   20   15   30   20   40   25

kilometres

miles

Route description

TL out of car park onto B4348 (Oxford Road).

1 TR at TJ into Church Street, no SP. Then LHF, SP Hereford/A438.

2 TL over Hay Bridge and cross River Wye, SP Clyro B4351. Continue to Clyro.

3 TR at TJ and immediately TL into Clyro, SP Painscastle. Then TL, SP Painscastle.

4 TL, SP Painscastle, and climb. Cross cattle grid onto Begwyns – beware loose sheep. Continue towards Painscastle.

To visit Tawny Owl Animal Park TR on approach to Painscastle, SP Tawny Owl Animal Park, and immediately TL.

Otherwise, continue into Painscastle.

5 TR at TJ, SP Newchurch (9.5km/6 miles). Continue into Newchurch.

6 To take short cut, TR by church, SP Michaelchurch. Continue through Michaelchurch and rejoin route at direction 12, where TR, SP Brilley.

Otherwise, to continue route, TL by church, SP Glascwm. **_16.5km (10.5 miles)_**

7 TR at XR, SP Gladestry/Colva. Continue through Colva. Stay on this road (excellent views), ignoring all turnings, until arrive at TJ.

8 TL at TJ, SP Cycle Route 25 (25km/ 15.5 miles). Continue into Gladestry and pass Royal Oak on RHS.

9 TR after pub, SP Huntington.

10 TR, SP Huntington, and climb.

11 SO at XR, SP Brilley.

12 TL at TJ, SP Brilley.

13 TR at TJ, no SP (34.5km/21.5 miles). Continue through Brilley. Descend to TJ with A438.

14 TL at TJ, SP Hereford/A438.

15 TL onto B4350 (with CARE), SP Clifford, and cross River Wye via toll bridge (5p charge for bicycles). Continue into Hay-on-Wye. Stay on B4530 to arrive back at car park and the end of the ride. **_46.5km (29 miles)_**

Hay-on-Wye

ABERGAVENNY AND RAGLAN

Route information

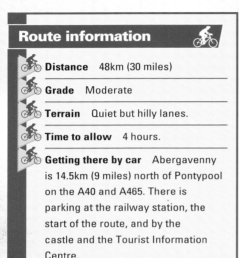

Distance   48km (30 miles)

Grade   Moderate

Terrain   Quiet but hilly lanes.

Time to allow   4 hours.

Getting there by car   Abergavenny is 14.5km (9 miles) north of Pontypool on the A40 and A465. There is parking at the railway station, the start of the route, and by the castle and the Tourist Information Centre.

Getting there by train   There is a railway station at Abergavenny (with bicycle lockers). See page 13 for travel information.

A pretty route through the countryside of south Wales, with lots of good views. From Abergavenny the route heads east to Llanwetherine. From here the route turns south to Raglan before turning north and returning to Abergavenny, using a short section of the National Cycle Network (NCR 42). There is an option short cut, bypassing Raglan and reducing the total distance to 24km (15 miles). Allow extra time to visit the places of interest.

Places of interest along the route

Ⓐ Abergavenny

A pleasant historical market town (Tuesday is market day) at the confluence of the Rivers Gavenny and Usk, surrounded by hills, with the imposing conical shaped Sugar Loaf hill to the west (596m/1955 feet), Skirrid Fawr (486m/1595 feet) to the east and Ysgyryd Fach (270m/886 feet) to the south east. Abergavenny is popular with visitors – the town sits on the eastern edge of the Brecon Beacons National Park, is close to the Monmouthshire and Brecon Canal and is on the route of the Lôn Las Cymru (the Welsh National Cycle Network). **Abergavenny Museum** is housed in the remains of a Norman castle and describes the history of the town from prehistoric times to the present day. Open March to October, Monday–Saturday 1100–1300 and 1400–1700, Sunday 1400–1700; November to February closes at 1600 and closed all day Sunday. Charge. Telephone (01873) 854282. For more information on Abergavenny contact the Tourist Information Centre or visit www.abergavenny.co.uk

Ⓑ White Castle, near Abergavenny

An earthwork stronghold, the castle was rebuilt in stone during the 12th and 13th centuries and the name comes from its original colour. The round towers, inner wall and moat survive and offer wonderful views. Cadw property. Open

White Castle

April to September, daily 1000–1700; telephone to confirm winter opening times. Charge. Telephone (01600) 780380; www.cadw.wales. gov.uk

C Raglan Castle, Raglan

Sir William ap Thomas began construction of the castle in 1435 and his son continued the work, creating a grand palace. Cadw property. Open March to May and October, daily 0930–1700; June to September closes 1800; November to March, Monday–Saturday closes 1600, Sunday 1100–1600. Charge. Telephone (01291) 690228; www.cadw.wales.gov.uk

Food and drink

Plenty of choice in Abergavenny and pubs and shops in Raglan. Note there are no opportunities for refreshment between Raglan and Abergavenny.

Kings Arms, Llanvetherine
Bar meals, tea and coffee and B&B.

Red Hart, Llanvapley
On the optional short cut. A cycle-friendly pub serving good food.

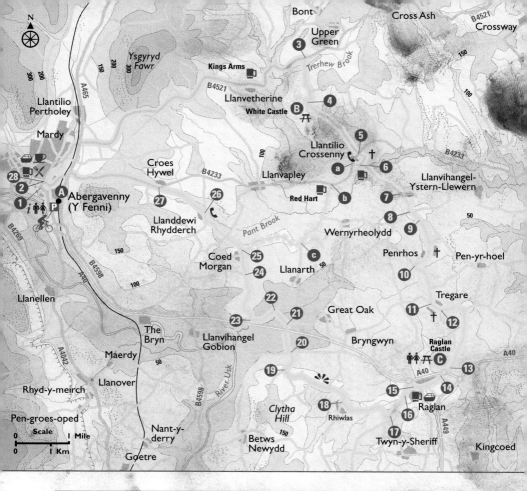

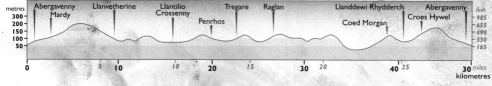

Route description

Leave Abergavenny railway station, cycle downhill to main road and TR to town centre (car park and Tourist Information Centre on RHS).

1 Follow road as it bears right, SP Brecon A40. SO through traffic lights, SP B4521/ Skenfrith.

2 TR (with CARE), SP Skenfrith/Hereford. Continue SO at XR, through Llandewi Skirrid and up through Llanvetherine.

3   TR, SP White Castle (12km/7.5 miles) and continue SO, SP White Castle, ignoring TL.

4   To visit White Castle, TR at TJ, SP Whitecastle.

Otherwise, to continue route, SO downhill to TJ.

5   TR at TJ onto B4233 (16km/10 miles).

To take short cut continue SO and:

a   SO at XR and ignore next TL.

b   TL, SP Llanarth. Over bridge and ignore next TL.

c   TR at XR, SP Coed Morgan. Continue on this road and rejoin route at direction 25, where TR downhill.

Otherwise, to continue main route, immediately TL and follow road to right, past church on LHS and telephone on RHS.

6   TL in front of Hostry Inn, SP Raglan/Penrhos. Continue over bridge.

7   TL at Y junction.

8   TL at TJ, SP Penrhos. Then TR at junction, SP Penrhos/Dingestow.

9   TR and continue SO into Penrhos village and past church.

10   TL at TJ (after church).

11   TL at TJ (23km/14.5 miles). Continue past Tregare church.

12   Bear L (after church). TR at next junction, SP Raglan.

13   TR at TJ and cross dual carriageway (with CARE), SP Raglan. Then TL, SP Raglan.

14   Take first TR (by bus stop and through 30mph SP). To visit Raglan Castle TR through gap in wall at SP roundabout (above on dual carriageway). Recross dual carriageway (CARE – walk bicycles across road) and continue into castle. After visit, retrace route to gap in wall, TR and continue into Raglan.

Otherwise, SO to continue route.

15   TR at XR and continue through village. TL by Crown pub.

16   TL at TJ.

17   TR, SP Rhiwlas/Clytha Hill. Continue into Rhiwlas.

18   TR at TJ (opposite Castle View Farm) – good views of Brecon Beacons on RHS. Continue SO to end of lane.

33km (20.5 miles)

19   TR at TJ down steep hill (SP Footpath by gate opposite).

20   SO at XR with main road and continue over dual carriageway.

21   TL at TJ (by bungalow, 35.5km/22 miles).

22   TL at TJ (pass old horse trough).

23   TR, SP Llanddewi Rhydderch.

24   TR at junction, SP Coed Morgan.

25   TL at TJ. Continue downhill and SO into village, SP Llandewi Rhydderch. Bear R past telephone box.

26   LHF and continue into Croes Hywel.

27   TL at TJ onto B4233, part of NCR 42 (43km/27 miles). Continue for long downhill into Abergavenny.

28   TL at TJ. Follow road round to left, SP Through Traffic, and retrace route back to station (on LHS) to finish the ride.

48km (30 miles)

A CIRCUIT OF THE SUGAR LOAF MOUNTAIN

Route information

Distance 54.5km (34 miles)

Grade Strenuous

Terrain Well-surfaced, undulating roads with some stiff climbs. Suitable for more experienced cyclists on bicycles with low gears.

Time to allow 5 hours.

Getting there by car Abergavenny is 14.5km (9 miles) north of Pontypool on the A40 and A465. There is parking at the railway station, the start of the route, and by the castle and the Tourist Information Centre.

Getting there by train There is a railway station at Abergavenny (with bicycle lockers). See page 13 for travel information.

A circuit around the Sugar Loaf mountain in the Brecon Beacons National Park. From Abergavenny the route heads south to Blaenavon and then on to Brynmawr. From here you turn north, through the beautiful gorge of Clydach and on through Llanelly and the old limestone mining village of Llangattock to Crickhowell. From here the route circuits the northern side of the Sugar Loaf mountain and returns to Abergavenny.

Places of interest along the route

A Abergavenny

A pleasant historical market town (Tuesday is market day) at the confluence of the Rivers Gavenny and Usk, surrounded by hills, with the imposing conical shaped Sugar Loaf hill to the west (596m/1955 feet), Skirrid Fawr (486m/1595 feet) to the east and Ysgyryd Fach (270m/886 feet) to the south east. See route 14 for more information.

B Blaenavon

This area of south Wales saw much development during the Industrial Revolution and Blaenavon was at the centre of coal and iron production. **Blaenavon Ironworks** is one of Europe's best-preserved 18th-century ironworks. Dating from 1788, the furnaces here were, at the time, the latest technology, powered by steam engines rather than by waterwheels. Visitors can still trace the entire process of production and see the cottages built for the workers. Cadw property. Open Easter to October, daily 0930–1630. Charge. Telephone (01495) 792615; www.cadw.wales.gov.uk. Blaenavon pit was sunk in 1880 and closed in 1980. Today known as the **Big Pit**, visitors can descend underground into the original mine workings and explore the colliery buildings on the surface. Tearoom and gift shop. Open March to November, daily 0930–1700; telephone to confirm winter opening times. Charge. Telephone (01495) 790311.

ⓒ Crickhowell

Crickhowell sits on the River Usk and is dominated by Table Mountain (451m/1480 feet) to the north. The bridge over the river is curious – after being rebuilt in the 18th century, there are 13 arches on one side, but only 12 on the other. Alisby's Castle is the scant remains of the original 13th-century castle, with only the gatehouse tower and portcullis gate surviving. An interesting town trail describes many of the fine buildings. For more information, contact Crickhowell Tourist Information Centre.

Food and drink

Lots of choice in Abergavenny and Crickhowell. Brynmawr has a café and shops and refreshments are also available at the Big Pit.

🍽 **Whistle Inn, near Blaenavon**
Bar meals available.

☕ **Queens Coffee Tavern, Crickhowell**
Cyclists welcome. Open daily for snacks and light meals, and for fans of Cliff Richard – pictures of him decorate the interior and the menu.

Route description

Leave Abergavenny railway station, cycle downhill to main road and TR to town centre (car park and Tourist Information Centre on RHS).

1 TL into Castle Street (narrow street as main road bears right), SP Castle/car park. Then, TL at junction to see castle, or, TR at junction past car park and continue SO.

2 TL at junction.

3 TL at roundabout, SP Llanfoist/A4143. Cycle over river and TL at next roundabout, SP Llanfoist. Continue SO past Safeway into Llanfoist.

4 SO, SP Govilon, and continue under bridge.

5 TL, SP Blaenavon/Big Pit. Continue over canal and follow road, SP Big Pit, for long hard climb. Then SO at XR, SP Blaenavon (keepers pond and masts on LHS – 9.5km/6 miles). Continue, with CARE, for long steep descent into Blaenavon.

6 To visit Big Pit, SO at Texaco garage, SP Varteg/Pontypool. Pass Blaenavon Ironworks on RHS. Continue downhill and TR, SP Kays & Keas/Gilchrist Thomas Industrial Estate. TL then SO at XR and under bridge, SP Big Pit. TR, SP Big Pit and TR into car park. After visit, TR out of car park and immediately TL towards gates with warning SP Guard Dogs on Patrol. Go though gates and along old road past Blaenavon Steam Railway. Cross railway line, head towards houses and follow cycle path to Whistle Inn. TL onto B4248 and continue towards Brynmawr and direction 7.

Otherwise, TR at Texaco garage, SP Brynmawr B4248. SO past SP Steam Railway and continue on this road passing Whistle Inn on LHS. Ignore SP to Llanelly Hill and continue downhill into Brynmawr.

7 TR at roundabout, SP Merthyr/Abergavenny, and continue under footbridge.

8 To visit Brynmawr (café/shops), TL at roundabout, SP Beaufort/A4047. Continue to

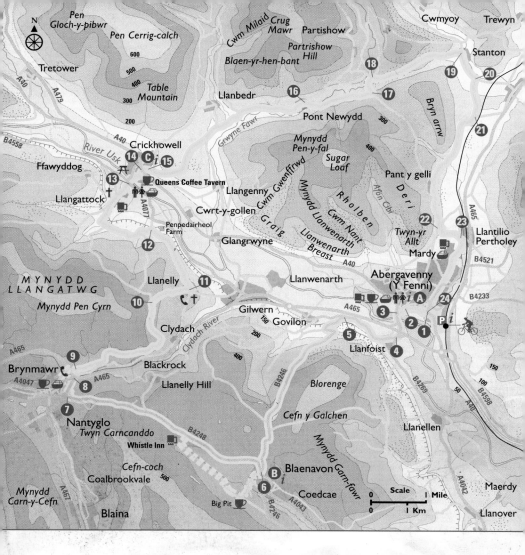

Pen Gloch-y-pibwr

Pen Cerrig-calch

Cwm Milaid   Crug   Partishow
                  Mawr

Partishow Hill

Blaen-yr-hen-bant

Cwmyoly   Trewyn

Stanton

N

Tretower

600

500

400

300

200

Table Mountain

Llanbedr

(18)

(16)

(17)

Pont Newydd

300

Bryn arrw

(19)

(20)

A40

A479

B4558

River Usk

A40

Crickhowell

(14) C i (15)

Mynydd Pen-y-fal

Sugar Loaf

Pant y gelli

(21)

Grwyne Fawr

400

Deri

Ffawyddog

(13)

Queens Coffee Tavern

Cwm Gwenffrwd

Rholben

(22)

Llantilio Pertholey

Llangattock

Penpedairheol Farm

(12)

Llangenny

Cwrt-y-gollen

Graig

Cwm Nant

Mynydd Llanwenarth

Twyn-yr Allt

(23)

Glangrwyne

Llanwenarth Breast

Mardy

B4521

MYNYDD LLANGATWG

Llanelly

(11)

A40

Mynydd Pen Cyrn

(10)

Llanwenarth

Abergavenny (Y Fenni)

(24)

B4233

Gilwern

150

Govilon

A465

(3)

A

(2)

(1)

P i

Clydach

Clydach River

200

(5)

Llanfoist

(4)

150

100

A465

(9)

Blackrock

400

Llanellen

50

B4269

Brynmawr

A4047

(8)

Llanelly Hill

B4246

Blorenge

B4598

Nantyglo

Twyn Carncanddo

B4248

Cefn y Galchen

Mynydd Garn-fawr

Llanellen

A4042

Maerdy

Whistle Inn

Cefn-coch

Coalbrookvale

500

B

Blaenavon

i

Coedcae

Scale

1 Mile

Llanover

Mynydd Carn-y-Cefn

Blaina

Big Pit

(6)

B4246

A4043

0   1 Km

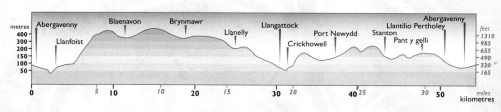

metres		Abergavenny		Blaenavon		Brynmawr			Llanelly	Llangattock			Stanton	Llantilio Pertholey	Abergavenny	feet
400			Llanfoist								Port Newydd		Pant y gelli			1310

metres
400
300
200
150
100
50

Abergavenny
Llanfoist
Blaenavon
Brynmawr
Llanelly
Llangattock
Crickhowell
Port Newydd
Stanton
Llantilio Pertholey
Pant y gelli
Abergavenny

feet
1310
985
655
490
330
165

0   5   10   15   20   25   30   50
                 10   20   30   40   50
                                                                 miles
                                                              kilometres

telephone box on RHS and TR over bridge and main road and TL at direction 9.

Otherwise, to continue route, SO at roundabout.

9 TR by factory (industrial complex) and continue past factories along disused Darren tramline (small memorial tramwheel on RHS). Continue along this level road (Clydach Gorge on RHS). Pass Old Grouse House and:

10 TR, no SP, down narrow lane past Pen yr Heol Farm (potholes and debris on road after heavy rain) to Llanelly Church and telephone box.

11 TL and TL again along lane.

27km (17 miles)

12 TL at TJ by Penpedairheol Farm, SP Wern Riding Centre. Cycle down hill, ignoring all TL, and follow road through SP 30 MPH, over canal into Llangattock. Follow SP Crickhowell through village and to main road.

13 TL at TJ. Then TR at traffic lights, SP Crickhowell/Brecon. Continue over river bridge into Crickhowell (picnic tables on LHS) and follow SP Brecon past church.

14 TR at TJ, SP Abergavenny/A40. Keep L towards Abergavenny over zebra crossing (32km/20 miles). TL, SP Car Park.

15 TR at mini roundabout and SO, SP Llangenny/Llanbedr. Continue along this road, SP Llanbedr/Fforest. Over bridge and SO, SP Fforest.

16 TR, SP Fforest/Abergavenny.

17 TL at junction surrounding house (SP 50m ahead is broken off). TL at TJ at end of house and pass Nantddu cottage.

18 TR at XR, SP Cwmyoy/Llanthony/Capel-y-ffin, and continue towards Stanton.

19 TR at TJ, SP Llanvihangel/Abergavenny.

43km (27 miles)

20 TR after farm buildings.

21 TR at junction, SP Pant y gelli/Abergavenny/NCR 42. Continue through Pant y gelli.

22 TL into lane and TR at TJ.

23 TR at XR and through Mardy (pubs/shops). Continue along this road into Abergavenny. SO at traffic lights, SP Monmouth/A40.

24 TL at TJ in front of Angel Hotel, SP Through Traffic, and return to railway station and the end of the ride.

54.5km (34 miles)

LLANDOVERY AND PUMSAINT

Route information

Distance 66km (41 miles)

Grade Moderate

Terrain Generally well-surfaced minor roads and a short stretch of A road. A couple of hard climbs.

Time to allow 3–4 hours.

Getting there by car Llandovery is 27km (17 miles) west of Brecon on the A40, A89 and A4069. There is car parking in town.

Getting there by train Llandovery is served by four trains a day. See page 13 for travel information.

A route around eastern Carmarthenshire. From Llandovery the route heads south along the Tywi Valley to Llandgadog before turning north west to Talley and the surrounding beautiful countryside. On through Pumsaint and the route loops, with a steep climb and descent, to the River Cothi. There is an optional visit to the scenic Llyn Brianne Dam and Reservoir before the route heads south back to Llandovery.

Places of interest along the route

A Llandovery

small market town at the confluence of the vers Bran and Gwydderig and 2km (1 mile) ve the confluence of the Rivers Bran and

Tywi (the town's name means church amid the waters). There has been a settlement here since Roman times and there are still the scant remains of a Norman Castle in the town centre. The town lies between the Brecon Beacons and the Tywi Valley and the **Heritage Centre**, Kings Road, describes the history and legends of the Tywi Valley. Also information on seeing Red Kites, Brecon Beacons National Park and Tourist Information Centre. Open Easter to September, daily 1030–1300 and 1400–1700; October closes at 1600. Donation requested. Telephone (01550) 720693.

B Talley Abbey, near Llandeilo

By the Talley Lakes and the village of the same name, the abbey was originally founded circa 1180. Today only part of the abbey church and the cloister remain. However, this is a beautiful and peaceful site. Good picnic spot. Cadw property. Free access at all reasonable times. Telephone (02920) 500200; www.cadw.wales.gov.uk

C Pumsaint

The hamlet of Pumsaint lies in the Cothi Valley and is part of the Dolaucothi estate, owned by the National Trust. The Red Kite has survived in this area and there is a **Red Kite Information Point** in the village's old coach house, with displays on the oak woods, a traditional Red Kite nesting site. For more information on Red Kites, telephone (01558) 650707 or visit www.kitecountry.co.uk. **Dolaucothi Gold Mines** were first mined over 2000 years ago by the Romans. Visitors can tour the underground workings, or enjoy walks above ground. Also exhibition, shop and café. National Trust property. Open April to September, daily 1000–1700. Charge. Telephone (01558) 650359; www.nationaltrust.org.uk.

Llyn Brianne

Food and drink

Plenty of choice in Llandovery. There are pubs and, occasionally, convenience stores in the villages passed through en route, and refreshments are available at Dolaucothi Gold Mines. However, cyclists should not rely on being able to obtain refreshment en route and should carry food and drink to sustain them during the ride.

Edwinsford Arms, Talley
Bar meals available; set lunch served Sunday lunchtime; closed Monday lunchtime.

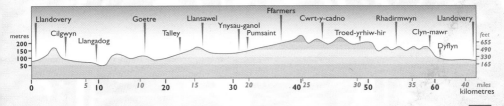

Route description

Leave railway station and TR onto A40 for 200m. Then TR, SP Llangadog/A4069.

1 TL onto minor road and follow this road towards Llangadog.

2 TL at TJ and TR onto A4069 through village to XR with A40.

3 SO at XR, no SP. Continue on minor road.

4 TR at TJ, SP Talyllchau/Talley.

5 TL then TR at staggered XR, SP Talley.

6 TR at TJ onto B4302, no SP (16km/10 miles). Continue through Talley, abbey on LHS, pub on RHS.

7 TL, SP Llansawel/B4337, for stiff climb into Llansawel.

8 TR at TJ, SP Pumsaint/Llanwdra.

25.5km (16 miles)

9 TL, no SP.   *27km (17 miles)*

10 TL at TJ onto A482. Continue through Pumsaint.

11 TR at TJ, SP Ffarmers (35.5km/22 miles). Continue into Ffarmers (Shackles Ddol in village repairs bicycles).

12 TR at TJ, SP Cwrt-y-cadno. Continue for stiff climb and descent (CARE). Continue into Cwrt-y-cadno.

13 TL at TJ, SP Rhandirmwyn (43km/27 miles). Continue to TJ by bridge.

14 TL at TJ over bridge (53km/33 miles). To visit Llyn Brianne Dam and Reservoir (excellent views/scenery) TL.

Otherwise, continue SO through Rhandirmwym and stay on this road back into Llandovery.

15 TR at TJ, SP A40. Continue to TJ with A40 where cross road to arrive at station and end of ride.   *66km (41 miles)*

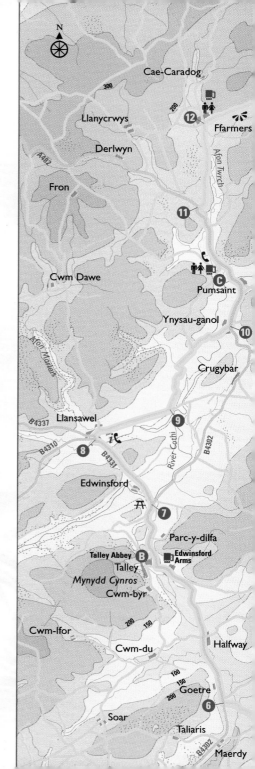

BRECON, UPPER CHAPEL AND BUILTH WELLS

Route information

Distance   69km (43 miles)

Grade   Strenuous

Terrain   Mainly quiet lanes and B roads. The return route between Builth Wells and Upper Chapel crosses an artillery range and access can be delayed for up to 15 minutes if firing is taking place – a warning sign is erected. There is a long, steep climb between Builth Wells and Upper Chapel.

Time to allow   3–6 hours.

Getting there by car   Brecon is 22.5km (14 miles) from Merthyr Tydfil on the A40 and A470. This route starts from the Canal Street car park.

Getting there by train   The nearest railway station is at Builth Road, close to Builth Wells.

This route can be accessed by bus – the Breacon Bike Bus runs from Cardiff. Telephone Cardiff Tourist Information Centre (see page 13) for more information.

A figure of eight from Brecon to Upper Chapel, and on to Builth Wells and back. Two shorter options can be followed: by cycling the loop between Brecon and Upper Chapel (35.5km/ 22 miles, moderate); or by starting from Builth Wells and making a loop to Upper Chapel and back (33km/20.5 miles, strenuous). The route takes you through the scenic Brecon Beacons with panoramic views over Powys, and includes a section of the National Cycle Network (NCR 43).

Places of interest along the route

A Brecon

Brecon is a small market town at the confluence of the Rivers Honddu and Usk, within the Beacons National Park. This area has been inhabited for thousands of years and there are ancient British and Roman remains close by. Brecon Cathedral is over 900 years old. The **Cathedral and Heritage Centre**, Cathedral Close, explains the history of the building. Also traditional hay meadow and 16th-century tithe barn. Tearoom. Open all year, Monday–Saturday 1030–1600. Admission free. Telephone (01874) 625222. **Brecknock Museum**, Captains Walk, describes local history and archaeology and holds regular exhibitions. Open all year, Monday–Friday 1000–1700, Saturday 1000–1300 and 1400–1700 (November–February closes 1600); Sunday 1200–1700 (April to September only). Telephone (01874) 624121. Brecon is the present terminus of the Monmouthshire and

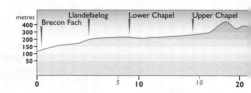

Brecon Cathedral

Brecon Canal and is on the National Cycle Route. For more information about Brecon, contact the National Park/Tourist Information Centre (see page 13), or visit www.brecon.co.uk

B **Builth Wells**

Builth Wells is former spa town on the River Wye. There has been a settlement here since Norman times, when a castle was constructed to guard a crossing of the River Wye and the entrance to the Irfon valley. Today only the remains of the Norman motte and bailey can be seen. The discovery of mineral water springs made the town popular during Victorian times, when the railway reached Builth. Today Builth Wells is well-known for its show grounds, just to the north of the town, which hold prestigious annual shows.

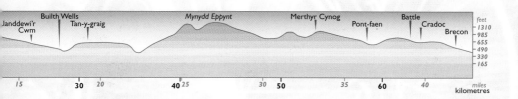

Route description

To start from Builth Road Station, TR from station onto A470. Pass Royal Welsh Show ground on LHS and follow SP Builth Wells. Cross river and TR into one-way system, SP Town Centre. Pass car park beside river, then pass Cosy Corner Tearoom on RHS and continue SO to join route at direction 6.

To start from Brecon, TR out of Canal Street car park. TL at mini roundabout.

1 TL at TJ and follow one-way system to Town Centre. Take LHF, SP Llandovery.

2 SO at traffic lights into High Street Superior, no SP.

3 TL, SP Upper Chapel, and climb past cathedral on RHS. Continue on this road into Upper Chapel. *15km (9.5 miles)*

4 To shorten the route (bypassing Builth Wells and returning to Brecon), TL by church, SP Merthyr Cynog and continue to direction 11.

Otherwise, to continue to Builth Wells, SO through village and continue on this road for climb then long descent (CARE – steep descent and sheep) into Builth Wells.

5 To visit town centre, follow one-way system, SP Town Centre. Continue along one-way system to rejoin route.

Otherwise, TL at TJ opposite opposite Cosy Corner Tearoom, no SP (28km/17.5 miles).

6 TL into Hospital Road, SP Cycle Route 43, for gradual climb.

7 RHF, SP Llangammarch/Cycle Route 43. *30.5km (19 miles)*

8 TL at XR, SP Upper Chapel/B4519. A warning SP is displayed by cattle grid at foot of climb if road is temporarily closed during firing. If SP is displayed, DO NOT proceed until it is removed. Climb from cattle grid, past viewpoint and, ignoring all turnings, descend to TJ.

9 If you are riding the shorter loop from Builth Wells, TL, SP Builth Wells. Climb and descend and follow one-way system through town centre to complete ride at car park. Or continue through town and retrace route to railway station.

Otherwise, to continue main route, TR at TJ, SP Brecon/Upper Chapel. Descend to Upper Chapel.

10 TR, SP Merthyr Cynog (48km/30 miles). Continue into Merthyr Cynog.

11 LHF, SP Pontfaen. *53km (33 miles)*

12 LHF, SP Brecon. Descend through Pontfaen and Battle into Cradoc.

13 SO at XR, SP Brecon, and continue into Brecon.

14 TL at TJ, no SP, and SO at traffic lights. Follow one-way system to Canal Street car park and the end of the ride. *69km (43 miles)*

If you started from Builth Wells, TL at traffic lights into High Street Superior and continue route from direction 2.

Food and drink

There are plenty of cafés and pubs in Brecon and Builth Wells. However, there are no shops, cafés or pubs en route so cyclists should carry food and drink to sustain them during this strenuous ride.

THE GOWER PENINSULA

Route information

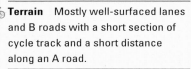

 Distance 72.5km (45 miles)

Grade Moderate

Terrain Mostly well-surfaced lanes and B roads with a short section of cycle track and a short distance along an A road.

Time to allow 5–6 hours.

Getting there by car Gowerton is 8km (5 miles) north west of Swansea. From the M4 take the A483 (junction 47). Then take the A484 and the B4296 to Gowerton. From Swansea take the A483 and the B4295. Park in Sterry Road car park (on the B4295, just after Ty Gwyn Mawr pub).

Getting there by train Gowerton has a railway station. See page 13 for travel information.

A route around the Gower Peninsula, a designated Area of Outstanding Natural Beauty. From Gowerton the route heads south to Mumbles and Mumbles Head. Turning west, the route runs along the southern side of the Gower, through Bishopston, Nicholaston and Oxwich before turning north, heading up to Cheriton and turning back to Gowerton. See also route 5 for more details on the Gower Peninsula.

Route description

From Gowerton Station, walk along Station Road to Sterry Road and car park on RHS.

From car park, cross Sterry Road into Woodlands Terrace (opposite) and continue to end.

1   Join cycle path. Continue to end of housing estate (end of cycle track) and continue SO. Then, TR, after SP Gower Rise, and rejoin cycle track. Continue to seafront.

2   To visit Oystermouth Castle, TR along A4067 and follow SP Oystermouth Castle.

Otherwise, to continue route, cross A4067, bear L and TR over bridge (staying on cycle track).

3   Cycle track joins road at Mumbles Yacht Club. Bear L onto road.   ***11km (7 miles)***

4   TR into Plunch Lane.

5   TL, SP Gower/Caswell Bay.

6   TL, SP Bishopston (18.5km/11.5 miles). Continue into Bishopston.

7   TL, SP Port Eynon. Continue to Beaufort Arms pub.

8   TR by pub into Kittlehill Avenue.

9   TL at TJ onto A4118, no SP (23km/14.5 miles). Pass Gower Heritage Centre on RHS and continue through Nicholaston.

Oxwich Bay

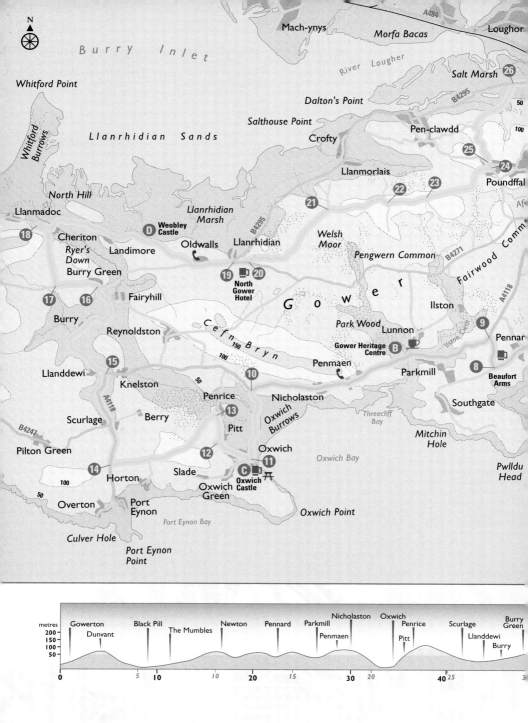

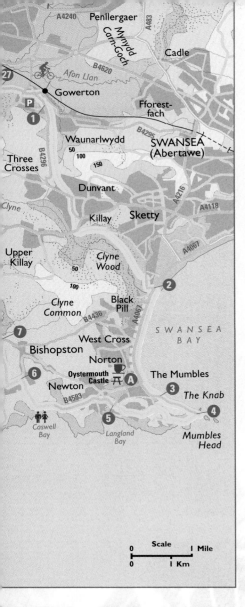

10 TL, SP Oxwich/Slade (32km/20 miles). Continue along this road, passing Oxwich Nature Reserve on LHS.

11 To visit Oxwich Castle, continue SO.

Otherwise, to continue route, TR, SP Penrice.

12 TR, SP Penrice.

13 TL, SP Horton.

14 TR onto A4118, no SP.

41.5km (26 miles)

15 TL, SP Burry Green, and continue into Burry Green.

16 TL, SP Llangennith.

17 TR, SP Llanmadoc. *50.5km (31.5 miles)*

18 TR, SP Llanrhidian/Cheriton. Continue through Cheriton, past Weobley Castle on LHS and into Llanrhidian.

19 TR onto B4271, SP Swansea.

58.5km (36.5 miles)

20 TL, SP Welsh Moor.

21 TR at TJ, SP Cilonen.

22 LHF, no SP. *64km (40 miles)*

23 Continue SO.

24 TL at TJ, no SP.

25 TL at TJ, SP Gowerton.

26 TR at TJ onto B4295 and continue into Gowerton.

27 TR at TL (Brynmor Road). Continue through Gowerton to car park on LHS to finish the ride. *72.5km (45 miles)*

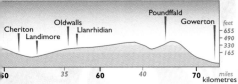

Places of interest along the route

A Oystermouth Castle, Mumbles

The remains of a 13th-century castle built on the site of an earlier wooden fortification. Visitors can enjoy wonderful views from the battlements. The surrounding grounds are a good picnic spot. Free access to grounds at all reasonable times. Castle open Easter to September, daily 1100–1700. Charge. Telephone (01792) 368732 or visit www.mumbles.co.uk

B Gower Heritage Centre

An award-winning centre based around a water-powered, 12th-century corn mill. Visitors can visit the restored mill and cottage. Also displays on the coracle, a reconstructed wheelwright shop, farm museum, mill leat and fish farm. Tearoom. Open all year, daily 1000–1730. Charge. Telephone (01792) 371206; www.gowerheritagecentre.sagehost.co.uk

C Oxwich Castle, Oxwich

This grand house was built during the 16th century, probably on the site of an earlier fortification. Some of the original six storeys still survive. Magnificent views of Oxwich Bay. Good picnic site. Open May to September 1000–1700. Charge. Telephone (01792) 390359; www.cadw.wales.gov.uk. The coast around Oxwich village is a nature reserve with many fine walks.

D Weobley Castle, near Llanrhidian

On the north coast of Gower, Weobley was built during the early 14th-century in a luxurious style and the remains are well-preserved Also exhibition on Gower's ancient monuments. Cadw property. Open daily, April to September 0930–1800; October closes 1700; November to March closes 1600. Charge. Telephone (01792) 390012; www.cadw.wales.gov.uk

Food and drink

There are a selection of cafés in Mumbles and several pubs passed en route serve food.

North Gower Hotel, Llanrhidian
Bar meals available.

Oystermouth Castle

TENBY, STACKPOLE AND PEMBROKE

Route information

Distance 72.5km (45 miles)

Grade Strenuous

Terrain Mostly quiet well-surfaced roads, with some challenging climbs and wonderful descents. The roads around Tenby, Manorbier, Stackpole and Pembroke can be busy during the summer.

Time to allow 6–8 hours.

Getting there by car Tenby is 14.5km (9 miles) east of Pembroke on the A478 and A4139. In the town, follow SP Station, where there is ample car parking.

Getting there by train There is a regular service to Tenby, with trains carrying either two or six bicycles. Cyclists should book their travel in advance. See page 13 for travel information.

A scenic route around the beautiful south Pembrokeshire coast. From the seaside resort of Tenby, the route heads west to the pretty village of St Florence. On to the quiet coastal villages of Manorbier and Freshwater East, before a climb through Stackpole, Bosherston and past Freshwater West beach. The route now follows undulating roads into Pembroke before a climb onto the Ridgeway for the return to Tenby. The route follows sections of the National Cycle Network (Celtic Cycle Trail). See also route 6 for information on St Florence and Manorbier.

Route description

TR out of Tenby Station car park and take next TR, SP Tenby Golf Club/Celtic Trail.

1 Cycle down hill and follow track between golf course and railway lines. TR over railway bridge and follow track into Kiln Caravan Park.

2 TL at road. Then TL at mini roundabout. Follow road out of Kiln Park to junction with A4139. TL and immediately TR, then TR again, SP St Florence. Continue into St Florence.

3 TL at TJ, past Flemish Chimney pub. TL at TJ (leaving Celtic Trail) down hill, SP Manorbier. Pass pub and village shop and follow road as it climbs (17%) to Ridgeway.

4 SO at XR at top of hill, SP Manorbier. SO at next XR, SP Manorbier. Continue into Manorbier.

5 Cycle through village, past village shop, Castle Inn and Chives Tearoom, and TL down hill, alongside castle. Follow this road as it rises beside beach (views of St Govan's Head ahead).

6 TL at TJ. Pass Swan Lake Tearoom. TL at TJ, then immediately TL into narrow lane SP Unsuitable for Vehicles. Continue into Freshwater East and pass pub.

7 Take first TL down sweeping hill and continue up other side into East Trewent.

8 Stay on this road and follow coastline. Pass TL, SP Barafundle (access to Stackpole Quay, tearooms and Barafundle Bay). Continue

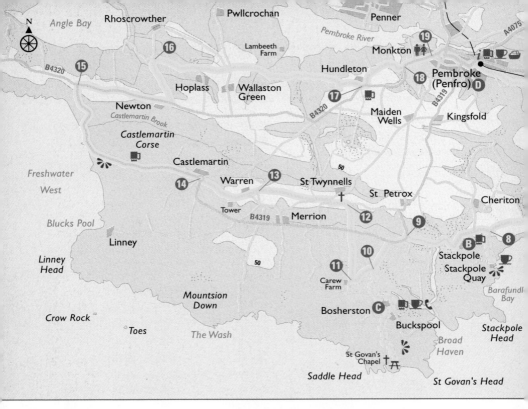

through Stackpole village, past pub and through woods (view of eight-arch bridge on LHS).

9 TL onto B4319 for approximately 0.5km (0.3mile), SP Bosherston. Then SO at junction leaving B4319. Continue for climb. At top of rise:

10 To visit Bosherston (tearoom, pub and access to lily pond, Broadhaven Beach and St Govan's Chapel), TL at top of rise, SP Bosherston.

Otherwise, TR, SP Carew Farm, and follow road to farm entrance.

11 RHF and continue to another farm and TJ where go SO, with CARE across busy road. Continue to top of lane.

12 TL. Ignore first TR then TR at TJ beside church, for short descent. TL and continue out of village. TR, SP Castlemartin/ Warren.

13 SO at XR. Pass Range Observation Tower (land on LHS is military firing range and if firing is taking place, this public tower enables visitors to watch the manoeuvres). Continue into Castlemartin.

14 TL at roundabout onto B4319 and cycle through Castlemartin. Descend and climb past Freshwater West beach.

15 TR at TJ, SP Pembroke. Take next TL, SP Rhoscrowther.

16 TR and follow ridge to TJ, where TR and take second TL to Lambeeth Farm.

17 SO into Hundleton. TL at TJ then TL by village green, out of village. TR into narrow lane (BEFORE you cycle down hill). Follow lane through woods and climb to TJ with main road.

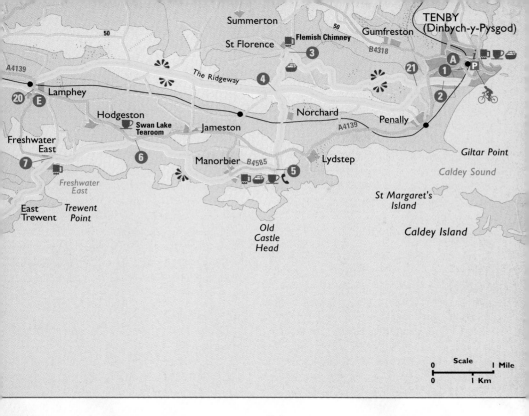

18 TL at TJ and continue through Monkton and into Pembroke, eventually cycling down hill in front of Pembroke Castle – look out for SP Celtic Trail.

---

19 TR, SP Celtic Trail, and follow trail through park. SO across road and follow trail to TJ, where TL then immediately TR. Continue to TR at TJ onto roundabout. Take third exit, down hill and follow Lower Lamphey Road into Lamphey.

---

20 TL at TJ, over railway bridge, and TR onto the Ridgeway. Follow Ridgeway towards Tenby (magnificent views of sea on RHS and Preseli Mountains on LHS). Ignore all turnings off this road and DO NOT follow SP Celtic Trail off to left. At end of ridgeway, road drops down to TJ.

21 TL at TJ. Then again TL at TJ and immediately TR into Kiln Caravan Park. Follow SP Celtic Trail. Take third exit and roundabout, TR up bank and cross railway bridge. TL between golf course and railway lines. Continue up hill, TL at TJ and follow road back to station and the end of the ride.

72.5km (45 miles)

Places of interest along the route

Ⓐ Tenby

Originally a medieval town, this popular seaside resort on the Carmarthen Bay has two expansive beaches to the north and south. The sparse remains of the town's castle are on a high rocky headland above the town, but some of the 13th-century town walls can still be seen. The **Tudor Merchant's House**, Quay Hill, is a fine example of how a wealthy family would have lived during Tudor times, when Tenby was a thriving port. Also herb garden. National Trust property. Open April to September, Monday–Saturday 1000–1700 (closed Wednesday), Sunday 1300–1700; October, daily except Wednesday and Saturday, 1000–1500, Sunday 1200–1500. Telephone (01834) 842279. Charge. For more information on Tenby visit www.virtualtenby.co.uk

B Stackpole

A popular village with a good pub, the Armstrong Arms. Much of surrounding Stackpole Estate is a designated area of Outstanding Natural Beauty, a Site of Special Scientific Interest and National Nature Reserve! The estate, National Trust property, comprises beaches, cliffs, grassland and dunes, lily ponds and woodland. Stackpole Quay was once the private harbour for the estate built to import coal for the mansion and export limestone from the local quarry. A footpath leads to beautiful Barafundle Bay. For more information, telephone the warden on (01646) 661359.

C Bosherston

This is the last village on the southern limits of Pembrokeshire. Part of the Stackpole Estate, the lily ponds can be approached from Bosherston car park, where there is also access to Broadhaven Beach. St Govan's Chapel, in the cliffs, was possibly built as a hermitage during the 13th century and today is still a peaceful and secluded place.

D Pembroke

A small town on the River Pembroke, dominated by **Pembroke Castle**, a 12th and 13th century fortress with a high Norman keep and the birthplace of Henry VII. Flint tools have been found on the site, suggesting that it was occupied during the Stone Age. Exhibitions and displays explain the local history. Snack bar open summer only. Open daily, April to September, 0930–1800; March and October, 1000–1700; November–February 1000–1600. Charge. Telephone (01646) 681510. Other attractions in Pembroke include the Tudor Merchant's House, the Museum of the Home and the Martello Gun Tower. Contact Pembroke Tourist Information Centre for more information (see page 13).

E Lamphey

Another pretty village. **Lamphey Bishop's Palace** was constructed during the 14th century and improved over the following 200 years. The palace had fishponds, fruit orchards, vegetable gardens and parkland. Today only ruins remains. Cadw property. Open all year, daily 1000–1700. Charge. Telephone (01646) 672224; www.cadw.wales.gov.uk

Food and drink

Plenty of choice in Tenby. Various teashops, pubs and convenience stores are passed along the way.

Bosherston ponds

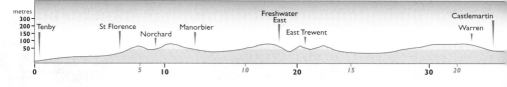

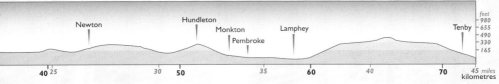

Route information

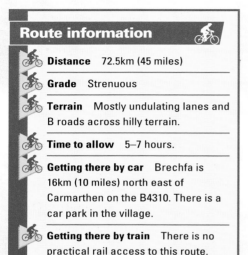

Distance 72.5km (45 miles)

Grade Strenuous

Terrain Mostly undulating lanes and B roads across hilly terrain.

Time to allow 5–7 hours.

Getting there by car Brechfa is 16km (10 miles) north east of Carmarthen on the B4310. There is a car park in the village.

Getting there by train There is no practical rail access to this route.

A scenic route through a remote and beautiful area. From Brechfa, at the centre of the Forest of Brechfa, the route heads north across Mynydd Llanbyther (402m/1319 feet) and Mynydd Pencarreg (415m/1361 feet) to the university town of Lampeter. From here the route turns south west to Llandysul in the Teifi Valley. On south to the hamlet of Llanpumsaint before returning to Brechfa. The route can be shortened, bypassing Llandysul and Llanpumsaint, to make a total distance of 61km (38 miles).

Places of interest along the route

Ⓐ Brechfa Forest

There are four waymarked mountain bike routes in the forest, designed for all levels of experience. Telephone Forest Enterprise on (01751) 472771 for more information.

Ⓑ Lampeter

Lampeter is a market town on the River Teifi. The University of Wales, originally St David's College, was founded here in 1822, the oldest college in Wales. During the 18th century the town was a gathering place for the drovers who herded Welsh livestock to the English markets during the 18th century. Market day is on alternate Tuesdays.

Ⓒ Rock Mill, Capel Dewi

Rock Mill was established in 1890 and is still owned by the same family. It is the last of the working water powered Welsh woollen mills. The mill manufactures blankets, throws, rugs and many other items. Open April to October, Monday–Friday 1000–1700, Saturday 1000–1300. Telephone (01559) 362356.

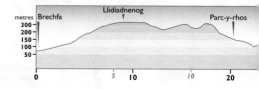

Route description

TR out of car park onto B4310.

1 TL, SP Gwernogle.

2 TR, SP Llidiadnenog. Continue through Llidiadnenog.

3 RHF, SP Llanybydder.

4 RHF, SP Rhydcymerau.   *9.5km (6 miles)*

5 TR at TJ, SP Llanllwni. Then TL, SP Llanybydder, and descend to B4337.

6 SO at XR, SP Parc-y-rhos, and LHF, no SP.

7 TR at Pant-y-fen Farm – do NOT go past telephone box on LHS (16.5km/10.5 miles). Continue to Parc-y-rhos, and descend to A485.

8 TR at TJ, no SP.   *21km (13 miles)*

9 TL at TJ onto A482, SP Lampeter. Cross River Teifi and continue into and through Lampeter.

10 TL onto A475, SP Newcastle Emlyn.

11 TR, no SP but immediately before derestriction SP, and climb.   *24km (15 miles)*

12 TL, no SP. Continue SO and descend.

13 SO at XR onto B4337, SP Llanbydder. Cross bridge and TR, SP Cwrt-newydd.
   29.5km (18.5 miles)

14 LHF (apparent SO) along minor lane, SP Cwrt-newydd.

15 SO at XR, SP Cwrt-newydd, and descend to B4338 in village.   *33km (20.5 miles)*

16 TR onto B4338. Then TL at XR, SP Newcastle Emlyn. Climb and continue to TJ with A475.

17 TR onto A475, no SP, and continue into Rhydowen.

18 TL at XR onto B4459, SP Capel Dewi. Continue into Capel Dewi (Rock Mill here).
   41.5km (26 miles)

19 To shorten route, continue on B4459 to Llanfihangel ar-arth.

a TL at XR, SP Lampeter/B4336. Continue to junction with A485.

b TL onto A485. Then TR, SP Rhos-y-corn.

c TR, SP Rhos-y-corn, and climb over Mynydd Llanfihangel.

d LHF, SP Brechfa, and descend to Brechfa to finish the ride.

Otherwise, to continue main route, TR at war memorial, SP Llandysul. Continue to junction with B4476.

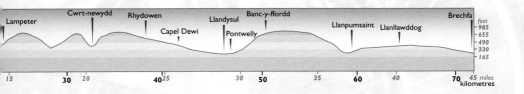

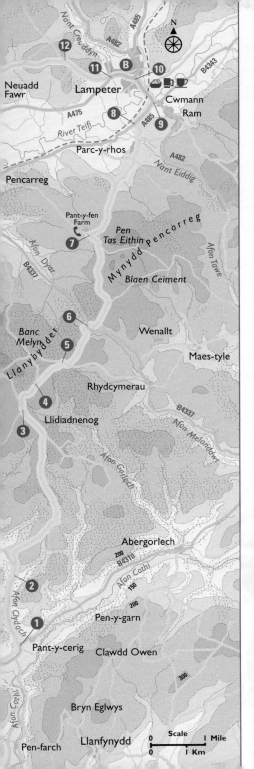

20 TL at TJ, no SP, and continue into Llandysul.

21 TL onto A486, SP Carmarthen. Continue into Pontwelly (ignoring junction with B4336).

22 TL opposite Half Moon pub, no SP (48km/30 miles). Continue for short, steep climb.

23 TR at TJ, no SP. Then TL, no SP, and continue climbing to Banc-y-ffordd (excellent views). Descend into Llanpumsaint and under disused railway.

24 TL, no SP.   *60km (37.5 miles)*

25 TL at TJ, no SP. Continue to next TJ.

26 TR at TJ, SP Alltwalis. Continue to A485.

27 TR at TJ onto A485. TL, SP Llanllawddog/Brechfa. Continue along this road, following SP Brechfa.

28 RHF, SP Brechfa. Descend into village. TL at TJ onto B4310 and continue to car park and the end of the ride.

72.5km (45 miles)

Food and drink

There are cafés, pubs and a super-market in Lampeter. However, this is a ride through a remote area and although there are are several pubs en route, they tend to close outside the holiday season. Cyclists can not rely on obtaining refreshment en route and should carry food and drink to sustain them during the ride.

NARBERTH, AMROTH, ST FLORENCE AND CAREW

Route information

Distance 74km (46 miles)

Grade Strenuous

Terrain Well-surfaced country lanes with challenging climbs and wonderful descents. Sections of route along the coast will be busy in the summer.

Time to allow 6–8 hours.

Getting there by car Narberth is 16km (10 miles) east of Haverfordwest and 14.5km (9 miles) north of Tenby on the A478. Follow the town's one-way system. At top of main street, take LHF and immediately TL into car park.

Getting there by train There is a railway station in Narberth. See page 13 for travel information.

From Narberth the route heads east along the Tavernspite Ridgeway, for stunning views over the entire county. On for a climb around the little known area of New Mill and onto a section of the National Cycle Network (Celtic Trail route 4) to the seaside resorts of Amroth and Saundersfoot. From here the route heads inland to St Florence and Carew, before returning to Narberth. The route can be shortened, bypassing the ridgeway and New Mill, making a total distance of 63.5km (39.5 miles).

Places of interest along the route

Ⓐ Narberth

A centre for antiques in Pembrokeshire. The town has many handsome Georgian houses and the remains of a 13th-century castle (not open to the public). The **Wilson Museum**, Market Square, explains the local history. Open all year, Monday–Friday 1030–1630, Saturday 1030–1230; Bank Holiday Monday 1030–1300. Charge. Telephone (01834) 861719.

Ⓑ Colby Woodland Gardens, near Amroth

Woodland and a walled garden in a secluded valley. National Trust property. Art gallery, plant sales and tearoom. Woodland open April to November, daily 1000–1700; walled garden open April to October, daily 1100–1700. Charge. Telephone (01834) 811885; www.nationaltrust.org.uk

Ⓒ Saundersfoot Bay Leisure Park, Saundersfoot

The leisure park (also a caravan park) has 8ha (20 acres) of landscaped gardens. Plant sales and woodland walk to beach. Open at most times in summer — telephone to confirm. Charge. Telephone (01834) 812284.

Ⓓ St Florence

A pretty village. See route 6 for details.

Ⓔ Carew

A picturesque village on the easterly tip of the Cleddau Estuary. See route 6 for more details.

Route description

If starting from Narberth Station, TL off platform, up hill and TL at TJ. Then TL at next TJ and join route at direction 1.

TR out of car park and TL at TJ, following one-way system east out of Narberth. Bear left as road splits and take sharp TL. Immediately TR and continue SO, SP Railway Station. Continue to Princes Gate XR.

1 SO at XR, SP Ludchurch, and continue up hill to XR.

2 To shorten route, SO at XR. SO at next XR. Pass Colby Woodland Gardens and continue up hill. TR and freewheel down hill to TR at TJ in Amroth. Continue along this road to rejoin main route at direction 10.

Otherwise, to continue route, TL at XR (5km/ 3 miles). Continue into Tavernspite.

3 TR (13.5km/8.5 miles) then take second TL, SP Llanddowror. Continue along ridgeway.

4 TR, by Cnwce House, down narrow lane and steep hill (CARE).

5 TL at TJ and immediately TR (CARE) across busy A477, SP New Mill (16km/10 miles).

6 TR at TJ, SP Pendine, and follow road through woods.

7 TR at TJ, SP Red Roses/Amroth (joining Celtic Trail).

8 SO at XR and follow SP Amroth/Marros.

9 TR at TJ , SP Amroth/Marros, down hill past pub then climb into Marros. Continue through Marros and Amroth (to visit Colby Gardens, TR and follow SP Colby Gardens) then SO into Summerhill.

10 TL in Summerhill (31.5km/19.5 miles). Continue to Wiseman's Bridge.

11 Two options to access Saundersfoot: dismount and follow Celtic Trail through tunnels to Saundersfoot; or, climb road into Saunders-foot. Follow one-way system in Saundersfoot. At foot of hill, by SP car park, TL then immediately TR along Brookland Lane. Follow lane to end and TL. TL again up sharp hill to XR.

12 SO at XR (CARE) across busy A478 into Devonshire Drive.

13 SO at XR.   ***40km (25 miles)***

14 TL at TJ and follow road into St Florence. Follow one-way system through village.

15 SO at XR (onto Celtic Trail), SP School.

16 TL at TJ, past Dingle Farm.

17 TL at TJ, up hill and onto Ridgeway.

18 TR at TJ, SP Lamphey/Pembroke.

19 TR, SP Milton, leaving Celtic Trail (47.5km/29.5 miles). Continue to TJ with A477.

20 TR at TJ onto A477 (CARE).

21 TL, SP Carew. Continue down hill, past pub and castle and over bridge.

22 TL, SP West Williamston. Continue to village, ignoring all junctions to right.

23 LHF to Cresswell Bay. TL at TJ to Cresswell Quay. Continue across bridge.

24 TR (just over bridge), SP Martletwy. Climb to top of hill and brown SP of grapes.

25 TR and continue to end of lane and junction with A477.

26 SO at XR (CARE), across A477, SP Jeffreyston. SO at next XR, SP Narberth. Continue to top of hill.

27 TL at top of hill, SP Narberth.

28 SO at XR, SP Narberth (64km/40 miles). Continue along this road, ignoring all turnings.

29 TL at TJ into Narberth. Finish the ride in the car park.   ***74km (46 miles)***

To return to railway station, follow one-way system and SP Station through town.

Food and drink

Plenty of choice in Narberth, Amroth and Saundersfoot.

Old Mill Café, near New Mill
Snacks and hot drinks available.

Bramleys Tearoom, St Florence
This tearoom has won prizes for its cakes.

Carew Inn, Carew
Good homemade meals.

Cresselly Arms, Cresswell
Popular pub serving food.

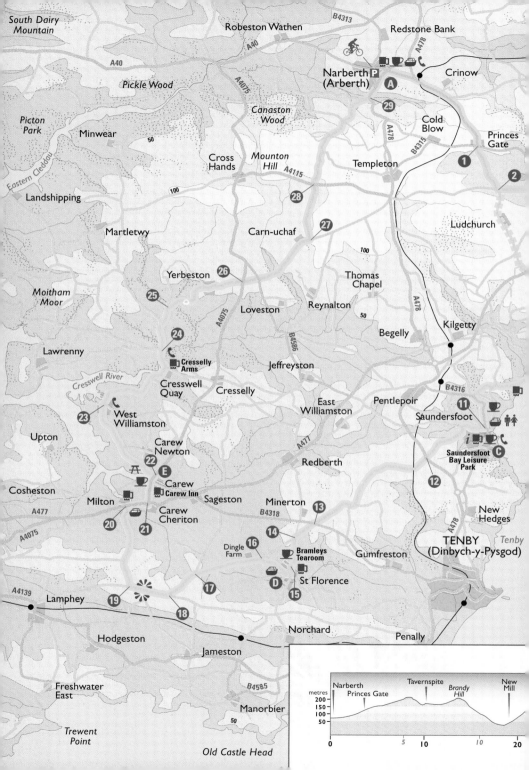

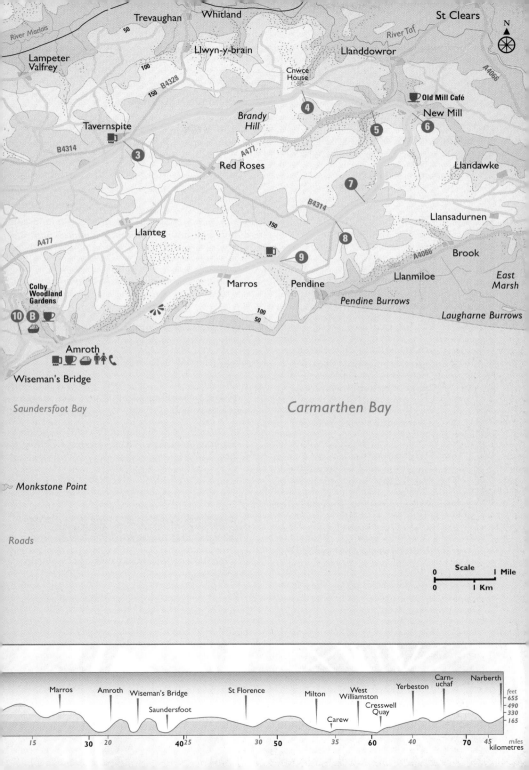

THE BRECON BEACONS NATIONAL PARK

Route information

Distance   83.5km (52 miles)

Grade   Strenuous

Terrain   Mostly quiet undulating lanes and two sections of quiet A road. There is a lot of climbing in this route, suitable for fit cyclists on bicycles with low gears.

Time to allow   4–8 hours.

Getting there by car   Brecon is 22.5km (14 miles) from Merthyr Tydfil on the A40 and A470. This route starts from the Canal Street car park.

Getting there by train   There is no practical rail access to this ride.

This route can be accessed by bus – the Beacon Bike Bus starts from Cardiff. Telephone Cardiff Tourist Information Centre (see page 13) for more information.

From Brecon the route follows quiet undulating lanes to Sennybridge and a brief section along the A40. A long climb offers spectacular views of the Black Mountains and the Brecon Beacons. The route descends to skirt the edge of the south Wales coalfield, now reclaimed,

planted and landscaped, before climbing and descending to the remote village of Ystradfellte. On for more climbing and a beautiful, winding descent. The final climb of the day takes you along Mynydd Illtyd for a long descent into Brecon. The route takes in mountains, woodland, caves and waterfalls, contrasting the bleak grandeur of the Black Mountains and the Brecon Beacons with the tranquil deciduous woodlands of the valleys. The woods are mainly a mixture of oak and birch rich in mosses, lichen and ferns, carpeted by a mass of bluebells in May. This route could be completed over two days (youth hostels at Ty'n-y Caeau, near Brecon, and Ystradfellte Youth Hostel – see page 13 for more information).

This route takes in remote areas. Cyclists should be well prepared. Check the weather forecast beforehand, particularly during winter and early spring as weather conditions can change rapidly. Carry suitable clothing to cope with the variable weather conditions, and food and drink for during the ride.

Route description

TR out of Canal Street car park and TL at mini roundabout.

1   TL at TJ and bear L into one-way system, SP Llandovery. Keep in L lane.

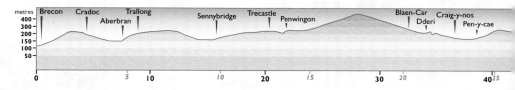

Henrhyd Waterfall

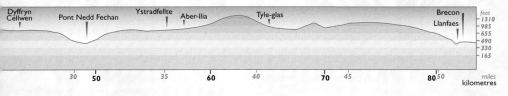

Dyffryn Cellwen   Pont Nedd Fechan   Ystradfellte   Aber-llia   Tyle-glas   Brecon   Llanfaes

feet
1310
985
655
490
330
165

30   50   35   60   40   70   45   80   50   miles
kilometres

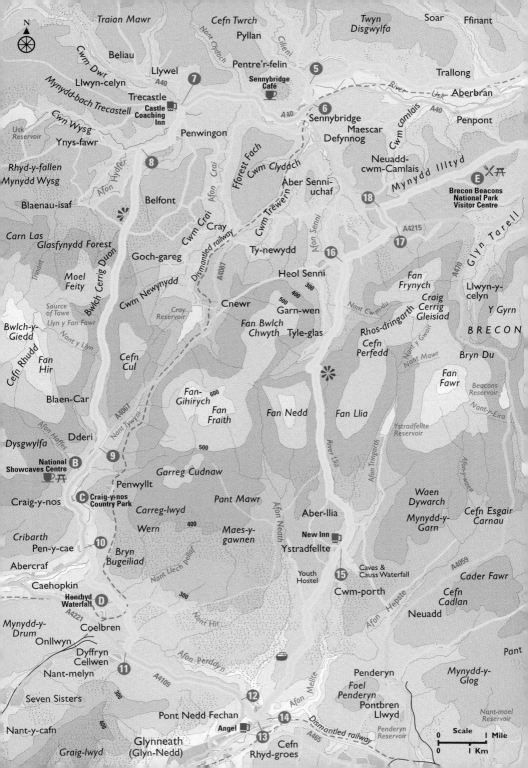

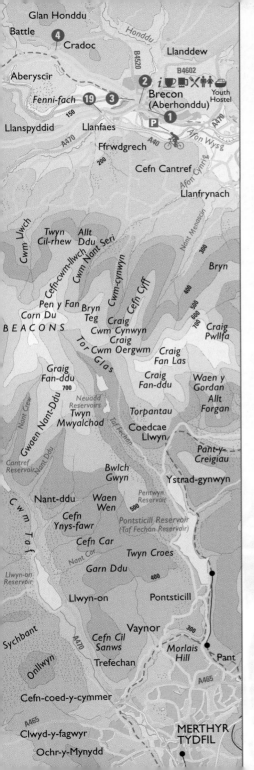

2 TL at TJ, SP Llandovery. Continue past Brecon Cycle Centre and:

3 TR, SP Cradoc. Continue into Cradoc.

4 TL, SP Aberbran. Continue through Aberbran, ignoring all turnings.

5 TL at TJ, SP Sennybridge. Continue and cross River Usk. **14.5km (9 miles)**

6 TR at TJ onto A40, no SP. Continue along A40 into Trecastle.

7 TL, no SP but immediately before Castle Coaching Inn.

8 TL, SP Abercraf. **24km (15 miles)**

9 TR at TJ onto A4067, SP Ystradgynlais/ A4067 (36km/22.5 miles). Continue along this road, past Showcaves on RHS and Craig-y-nos Country Park on LHS, and into Pen-y-cae.

10 TL, SP Henrhyd Waterfall (40km/ 25 miles). Continue, passing waterfalls on RHS.

11 TL at TJ onto Roman Road (A4109), no SP. Continue on this road and descend until about half-way down, by unsurfaced car park.

12 EASY TO MISS – TL by car park (if you arrive at sharp RH bend and foot of hill, you have gone too far). **49km (30.5 miles)**

13 Continue descent. To see River Mellte and ancient bridge, TR at TJ.

Otherwise, to continue route, TL at TJ (opposite toilets).

14 TL at TJ, no SP (49.5km/31 miles). Continue along this road, bearing L, SP Ystradfellte, and climb. Descend, passing Ystradfellte Youth Hostel on LHS and continue into Ystradfellte.

15 To visit caves/waterfalls, TR at three-way junction.

Otherwise, to continue route, TL at three-way junction, SP Sennybridge. Gradually climb following Riva Llia, before a long sweeping descent with hairpins (CARE) to Heol Senni.

16 TR at TJ, SP Brecon. *70km (43.5 miles)*

17 TL at TJ onto A4215, SP Defynnog.

18 TR at XR, no SP (73km/45.5 miles) and climb Mynydd Illtyd. To visit Mountain Centre, TR, SP Mountain Centre (75.5km/47 miles). Otherwise, continue SO and descend to round-about.

19 SO at roundabout, SP Brecon (82.5km/ 51.5 miles). Cross river, continue and TL into one-way system. Continue to Canal Street car park and finish the ride. *83.5km (52 miles)*

Places of interest along the route

For more information on the Brecon Beacons, contact Brecon Tourist Information Centre (see page 13) or visit www.brecon-beacons.com

Ⓐ Brecon
Brecon is a small market town at the confluence of the Rivers Honddu and Usk and north of the Brecon Beacons, part of the Brecon Beacons National Park. See route 17 for more information.

Ⓑ National Showcaves Centre, near Craig-y-nos
A site of Special Scientific Interest the centre comprises three stunning caves, a dinosaur park, replica Iron Age farm, shire horse centre, and Victorian Farm. Also museum, craft shop, tearoom and picnic area. Open April to October, daily from 1030, last admission 1500. Charge. Telephone (01639) 730801; www.show-caves.co.uk

Ⓒ Craig-y-nos Country Park, Penycae
Over 16ha (40 acres) of countryside in the Tawe Valley, including woodland, grassland, rivers, lakes and streams. Visitor Centre. Open all year, daily from 1000, closing times vary. Admission free. Telephone (01639) 730395.

Ⓓ Henrhyd Waterfall
A beautiful and spectacular waterfall with an unbroken drop of approximately 27m (90 feet), the highest waterfall in the Brecon Beacons National Park.

Ⓔ Brecon Beacons National Park Visitor Centre, near Libanus
This is the park's Mountain Centre, at 335m (1100 feet) above sea level. There are excellent views of Pen Y Fan, the highest mountain in south Wales. The centre offers information on all aspects of the National Park. Good value restaurant. Picnic area. Open daily, April, May, June and September, 0930–1700; July and August, closes 1800; November to March closes 1630. Admission free. Telephone (01874) 623366.

Food and drink

Plenty of choice in Brecon. Refreshments are available at the National Showcaves Centre and the National Park Visitor Centre.

🍵 Sennybridge Café
Hot drink and snacks served.

🍽 The Angel, Pont Nedd Fechan
Meals served at lunchtime.

🍽 New Inn, Ystradffellte
Food available at lunchtime.

HEREFORD, ROSS-ON-WYE AND MONMOUTH

Route information

Distance 93km (58 miles)

Grade Strenuous

Terrain Mostly quiet lanes and B roads with several steep climbs. There is a short section along a designated cycle route. The roads around Hereford can be busy.

Time to allow 6–9 hours.

Getting there by car Hereford is approximately 27km (17 miles) north of Monmouth, on the A438, A49 and A465. There is a long stay car park off the A438 (Bath Street) in the city centre.

Getting there by train There is a main line station at Hereford. See page 13 for travel information.

An interesting route with lots to see along the way. From Hereford the route heads south, through Ross-on-wye and down to Monmouth. From here you turn north and pass through Skenfrith and back to Hereford. The route offers excellent views of the Wye Valley, a designated Area of Outstanding Natural Beauty, and across Herefordshire.

Route description

From Hereford station, TL into Station Approach. TL at traffic lights into Commercial Road and cross railway.

TR out of Bath Street car park and TR at traffic lights (filter lane) into Commercial Road. Continue SO at traffic lights and cross over railway.

1 TR into Southbank Road, no SP.

2 SO at roundabout into Hafod Road, no SP.

3 TL at TJ onto B4224, no SP. Continue into Fownhope.

4 TR at XR, SP Capler, (11km/7 miles) for steep climb to Capler Camp viewpoint.

5 SO at XR, SP How Caple.

6 SO at XR, no SP, (16km/10 miles). Continue along lane, over cattle grid and follow River Wye through country estate (this is not a private road). Continue through Hole in the Wall and descend to Ross-on-Wye.

7 TR at TJ, then TL at next two mini round-abouts, SP Walford. ***24km (15 miles)***

8 Take fourth exit at roundabout, SP Walford, and TR in Town Centre, SP Walford. Then TL onto B4234, SP Walford, and continue.

9 TR and cross River Wye, SP Goodrich/B4229. Continue on B4229, passing entrance to Goodrich Castle on RHS.

10 TL, SP Symonds Yat (East).

32km (20 miles)

11 SO (effectively LHF), SP Yat Rock, and climb past Yat Rock.

12 TR at TJ, SP Coleford.

13 TR at XR, SP Monmouth (41km/ 25.5 miles). Descend to Monmouth (CARE long descent with hairpin bend at foot).

14 TR at TJ, SP Monmouth. Cross River Wye and SO at XR, SP Town Centre. Then TR at TJ, SP Town Centre. *49km (30.5 miles)*

15 TL at roundabout, SP Town Centre, and TL at XR, SP Town Centre/Hereford.

16 TL, SP Osbaston, and continue along this road.

17 TL at TJ, no SP (57km/35.5 miles) and cross River Monnow at Tregate Bridge. Climb to TJ.

18 TR at TJ, SP Skenfrith. Continue along ridge and descend to Skenfrith.

19 To visit Skenfrith Castle, TL at TJ onto B4521, no SP, and immediately TR.

Otherwise, TR at TJ onto B4521, no SP. Stay on this road through Broad Oak, SP Ross-on-Wye, and descend.

20 SO at XR, SP Ross-on-Wye. Continue to St Owen's Cross.

21 SO at XR, SP Ross-on-Wye.

72.5km (45 miles)

22 TR at TJ onto A49, SP Ross-on-Wye. TL at Winter's Cross, SP Sellack.

23 TL no SP.

24 TL at TJ, SP Hereford. Continue through Hoarwithy and climb, SP Hereford. Pass through Little Dewchurch.

82.5km (51.5 miles)

25 TL at roundabout into Holme Lacy Road, no SP (91km/56.5 miles). Take first TR, SP Cycle Route City Centre. TR at TJ, SP Cycle Route City Centre and follow cycle route through park to River Wye. TR and cross river via suspension bridge, SP Cathedral.

26 TL into Mill Street and LHF into Cantilupe Street. TR at TJ then immediately TR into Owen Street. TL at XR into Bath Street and retrace route to car park and the end of the ride. *93km (58 miles)*

To return to station, TR at XR (filter lane) into Commercial Street and continue to traffic lights where TL, SP Station.

Places of interest along the route

Ⓐ Hereford

A cathedral city on the River Wye. Hereford Cathedral dates from circa 1130 and is built on the site of an earlier Saxon church. The cathedral contains the Mappa Mundi, a medieval map of the world, and the Chained Library, a collection of 1400 chained books and

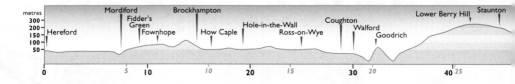

manuscripts dating from between the 8th and the 15th centuries. Open daily, summer Monday–Saturday 1000–1615, Sunday 1100–1515; winter Monday–Saturday 1100–1515. Charge. Telephone (01432) 374209. Other attractions include the city's Museum and Art gallery, the Waterworks Museum and the Cider Museum. Contact the Tourist Information Centre for more information (see page 13).

B How Capel Court, How Capel

Restored Edwardian gardens covering an area of 4.5ha (11 acres) high above the River Wye. Formal terraces, roses, water gardens and woodland walks. Open Easter to October, daily 1000–1700. Charge. Telephone (01989) 740626.

C Ross-on-Wye

A small market town on the River Wye, with a 17th-century market hall and many Georgian and timber-framed houses. Attractions include the Button Museum, the Lost Street Museum (a recreated Edwardian Street) and several craft shops. Contact the Tourist Information Centre for more information (see page 13).

D Goodrich Castle, Ross-on-Wye

The medieval castle is built an a rocky outcrop with exhilarating views over the Wye Valley. English Heritage property. Open daily, April to September 1000–1800; October closes 1700; November to March closes 1600. Telephone (01600) 890538; www.english-heritage.org.uk

E Symonds Yat, near Monmouth

A popular beauty spot on the River Wye with good views from Symonds Rock. A good picnic spot. Free access at all times.

F Monmouth

An interesting town with many attractions, in the heart of the Wye Valley, at the confluence of the Rivers Wye and Monnow. Building on Monmouth Castle started around 1068 and continued into the 14th century. The town's bridge over the River Monnow is topped by a gatehouse. Other attractions include the Nelson Museum, describing the life of Horatio Nelson. Contact the Tourist Information Centre for more information (see page 13).

G Skenfrith Castle, Skenfrith

The remains of a castle built by the Normans on one of the main routes between England and Wales. A good picnic spot. National Trust property. Free access at all reasonable times. For more information telephone (01492) 860123; www.nationaltrust.org.uk

Food and drink

Plenty of choice in Hereford and Monmouth.

Inn on the Wye, near Goodrich
Meals available.

Red Lion, Winters Cross
Bar meals available.

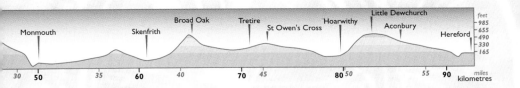

LLANELLI AND THE BLACK MOUNTAIN

Route information

Distance   120km (74.5 miles)

Grade   Strenuous

Terrain   Quiet minor roads, some short sections of busy A road and a section of the National Cycle Network (NCR 4).

Time to allow   1–2 days.

Getting there by car   Llanelli is 16km (10 miles) north west of Swansea on the A484, A476 and A4138, close to the the M4, junction 48. There is plenty of car parking in town, including a car park at the railway station.

Getting there by train   There is a station at Llanelli, on the south side of town. Trains stopping at Llanelli carry only two bicycles so cyclists should book their travel in advance. There are stations near Pontardulais and near Ammanford and Llandeilo, which could be used as alternative starting points.

Good views and lots to see along the way. The route starts from Llanelli and heads north to Ammanford and on around the base of the Black Mountain, reaching a height of 325m (1066 feet) above sea level, before arriving in Llandeilo. On along the Towy Valley, through the pretty Gwendrueth Fach valley to Llandy faelog and on to Ferryside on the coast. From here the route follows the coastline back to Llanelli.

Route description

TR out of railway station and TL into Copperworks Road/Marine Street.

1   SO at roundabout with B4304, join NCR 4 across road and TL (south). Continue along cycle route.

2   Rejoin road (7km/4.5 miles). To visit Penclawydd Wetlands and Wild Life Centre, TR.

Otherwise, TL to continue route. TR at round-about then SO at next roundabout, over bridge (CARE along this busy section of road).

3   TL at roundabout, SP Loughor.

4   TL at roundabout, SP Gorseinon/ Pontarddulais.

National Botanic Garden of Wales

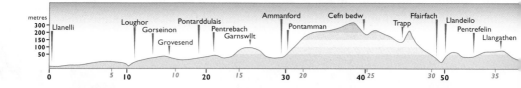

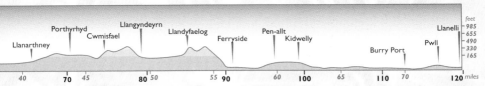

Llanarthney   Porthyrhyd Cwmisfael Llangyndeyrn Llandyfaelog Ferryside Pen-allt Kidwelly Burry Port Pwll Llanelli

feet
985
655
490
330
165

40   70 45   80 50   55 90   60 100   65   110 70   120 miles

5 TL at XR (traffic lights) into Frampton Road.

6 TL at TJ onto B4296 through Grovesend (16km/10 miles). Continue into Pontarddulais and SO at XR (traffic lights), SP Garnswllt.

7 TR at XR, SP Garnswllt. Continue into Ammanford, following SP Ammanford (29.5km/18.5 miles). In Ammanford TL at round-about.

8 TR at XR onto A474, SP Glanaman. Then SO at XR (traffic lights).

9 TL, SP Trapp.   *32km (20 miles)*

10 TR, SP Gwynfe/Heol Ddu, for stiff climb. SO at XR, SP Gwynfe (view west of Amman Valley). Continue and SO at XR, SP Gwynfe (view of Carreg Cennen Castle to north). Continue to reach a height of 325m (1066 feet) on this climb.

11 TL at TJ, SP Llandeillo. CARE on steep descent and then hard climb.

12 TL at XR, SP Carreg Cennen Castle (41.5km/26 miles). Continue, passing Carreg Cennen Castle and the Trapp Arts and Crafts Centre on LHS.

13 SO at TJ, SP Ffairfach, for stiff climb and fast descent.

14 TL at TJ, SP Ffairfach. *54.5km (34 miles)*

15 TR onto A483, SP Llandeillo, and continue into town.

16 To visit Dinefwr Park, TL.

Otherwise, SO to continue route.

17 TL, SP Llangathen. Continue on this road, passing Aberglasney Gardens on RHS.

18 To visit Gelli Aur Country Park, TR onto B4300.

To visit Llyn Lech Owain, TL onto B4297.

To visit Dryslwyn Castle, TR onto B4297 (good views but a stiff climb).

Otherwise, to continue route, SO on B4300 into Llanathnney.

19 TL, SP Porthyrhyd, for stiff climb (66km/41 miles). Pass access to Paxton's Tower on LHS. Then SO at TJ, SP Llanddarog (views east of National Botanic Gardens of Wales).

20 TL at XR, SP B4310/Porthyrhyd. Continue, passing entrance to National Botanic Gardens of Wales on LHS. Continue to Porthyrhyd.

21 Take second L at XR to stay on B4310 heading south for 200m, no SP (74km/46 miles). Then TR, no SP.

22 TR at TJ, SP Cwnsfail/ Llanddarog.

23 SO at TJ, SP Llangyndeyrn, and continue into Llangyndeyrn.

24 TR onto B4306 for 200m. Then TL, SP Pontantwn/Llandyfaelog.

25 TR onto B4309 and immediately TL, no SP (80.5km/50 miles). Continue for sharp climb to Llandyfaelog.

26 TL at TJ onto A484. Immediately TR, SP Ferryside. Continue through Ferryside and follow road along coast.

27   TR at TJ, SP Kidwelly.

28   TR at TJ (view of Kidwelly Castle).

98km (61 miles)

29   SO to visit Kidwelly Castle.

Otherwise, TR at TJ and continue through and out of Kidwelly.

30   To stay on road back to Llanelli (if time is short or the weather bad), continue along A484 into Llanelli.

Otherwise, to continue main route, join NCR 4 on RHS at SP (cycle route looks like pavement at this point, SP is further on). Stay on NCR 4, passing Pembrey Country Park (107km/ 66.5 miles). Continue through Burry Port and follow cycle route around harbour (stay on seaward side, along red tarmac) and continue past Millennium Coastal Path visitor centre.

31   Rejoin road at roundabout and SO, SP Railway Station. TL at TJ and TL into station to finish the ride.   *120km (74.5 miles)*

Places of interest along the route

Ⓐ Millennium Coastal Park, Llanelli

Twenty-two kilometres (13.5 miles) of coastline on the Burry Estuary, overlooking the Gower Peninsula, linked by a continuous traffic-free cycle and footpath. The park comprises wetlands and salt marshes, a floating harbour, beaches, sandbanks and woodland. For more information telephone (01554) 777744.

Ⓑ Penclawydd Wetlands and Wildlife Centre, near Llanelli

An award-winning visitor centre comprising 81ha (200 acres) of landscaped waterways with ducks, swans and geese. High rise observatory. Tearoom. Open all year, daily 0930–1700. Telephone (01554) 741087; www.wwt.org.uk

Ⓒ Carreg Cennen Castle, near Llandeilo

The castle is in a stunning location, on top of a limestone crag overlooking the Black Mountain. The ruins seen today date from the early 14th-century. A passage cut into the cliff leads under the fortifications to a natural cave which may have been inhabited in prehistoric times. Cadw property. Open daily, April to October 0930–1930; November to March 0930–dusk. Charge. Telephone (01558) 822291; www.cadw.wales.gov.uk

Ⓓ Trapp Arts and Craft Centre, Trapp

Welsh crafts and art gallery, and coffee shop. Changing demonstrations and exhibitions. Open March to Christmas, Tuesday–Sunday and Bank Holiday Mondays 1030–1800. Telephone (01269) 850175.

Ⓔ Dinefwr Park, near Llandeilo

A medieval castle, mansion house, gardens, woods and deer park. National Trust/ Cadw property. Tearooms (free access). Open April and October, Thursday–Monday 1100– 1700; May to September, daily 1100–1700. charge. Telephone (01267) 231817; www. nationaltrust.org.uk

Ⓕ Aberglasney, near Llangathen

Fascinating restored 16th- and 17th-century gardens. Tearoom. Open April to October, daily 0930–1800. Charge. Telephone (01558) 668998; www.aberglasney.org

G Gelli Aur Country Park, near Llandeilo

Gardens, nature trail, arboretum and deer park. Tearoom and picnic area. Telephone (01558) 668885 for opening times.

H Llyn Lech Owain Country Park, near Llandeilo

An area of 64ha (158 miles) comprising a lake, peat bog, woodland and heath. Waymarked paths and forest tracks. Visitor centre contains displays on local natural history and has live TV pictures from nest sites (between approximately April and August). Tearoom. Country park open daily, April to September 1000–2000; October to March closes 1600. Visitor centre open daily, April to September 1000–1700; October to March closes 1600. Admission free. Telephone (01269) 832229.

I Dryslwyn Castle, near Llanfihangel

The ruins of a medieval castle currently under excavation. On the banks of the River Tywi. Cadw property. Telephone (02920) 500200; www.cadw.wales.gov.uk

J Paxton's Tower

A viewpoint built in 1811 to commemorate the death of Horatio Nelson.

K National Botanic Garden of Wales, Llanarthney

The largest single span glasshouse in the world, with mediterranean garden, Welsh, British and European plants and much else. Café. Open daily, May to August 1000–1800; September and October closes 1730; November and December closes 1630. Telephone (01558) 667132; www.gardenofwales.org.uk

L Kidwelly Castle, Kidwelly

Well-preserved remains of a castle founded in 1106, rebuilt and completed in 1422. Overlooking the River Gwendraeth. Cadw property. Open daily, April and May 0930–1700; June to September closes 1800; October closes 1700; November to March, Monday–Saturday 0930–1600, Sunday opens 1100. Telephone (01554) 890104; www.cadw.wales.gov.uk

M Pembrey Country Park, Pembrey

Parkland and beaches covering an area of 202ha (499 acres), once the site of a Royal Ordnance Factory. Visitor centre, nature trails and other outdoor activities, including mountain biking. Café. Park open all year, daily dawn–dusk. Visitor centre open daily, April to August 1000–1700; September to March closes 1545. Free admission to park and visitor centre; charge for activities. Telephone (01554) 833913.

Food and drink

There are opportunities for refreshment in the towns and pubs passed along the way, and at most of the places of interest.

Golden Grove Arms, Llanarthney
Pub, restaurant and B&B.

Abadam Arms, Porthyrhyd
Meals served at lunchtime.

HEREFORDSHIRE AND THE WELSH BORDERS

Route information

 Distance   123.5 km (77 miles)

Grade   Moderate

Terrain   Mostly quiet lanes, with some climbing. The roads around Hereford can be busy. The route uses sections of the National Cycle Network.

Time to allow   1 or 2 days.

Getting there by car   Hereford is approximately 27km (17 miles) north of Monmouth, on the A438, A49 and A465. There is plenty of parking in town – the route starts from the car park off the A438, east of the junction with the A465.

Getting there by train   There is a main line station at Hereford. See page 13 for travel information.

A route through the Wye Valley and the Welsh borders, taking in Herefordshire and the Breacon Beacons National Park. From Hereford the route climbs and descends to Hay-on-Wye. A further climb and descent takes you to Llangorse and on to Crickhowell. The route continues along undulating roads and climbs up Campston Hill, with excellent views of the Black Mountains and across Herefordshire, before returning to Hereford along mostly flat roads. The route can be shortened by crossing the Black Mountains (total distance 98km/61 miles but strenuous).

Route description

If starting from Hereford railway station, TL out of station. Then TL, no SP.

Leave car park and TL onto A465. Cross railway and TL, no SP.

1   TL at mini roundabout, no SP. Then again TR at mini roundabout into Newtown Road, no SP.

2   SO onto A49 at mini roundabout (CARE). Then, TL, SP Brecon/A438.

3   TL at TJ, no SP.

4   TR at TJ, SP Burghill. Immediately TL, SP Burghill.

5   TL at TJ (Roman road). Immediately TR, SP Burghill.

6   TL at XR, SP Credenhill.

7   TR at TJ, SP Kington/A480.   ***7km (4.5 miles)***

8   TL, SP Bishopstone.

9   TR at TJ, SP Bishopstone.

10   TL at XR, SP Bridge Sollers.

12.5km (8 miles)

11   SO at XR (over A438), SP Preston on Wye.

12   TR, SP Preston on Wye (SP concealed in hedge). Continue through Moccas to XR.

13   TR at XR, SP Hay-on-Wye/B4352, (22.5km/14 miles) and continue into Hay-on-Wye (37.5km/23.5 miles).

14   TL at TJ, no SP. Continue out of Hay-on-Wye (route becomes NCR 48).

15   To take short cut, TL, SP Capel-y-ffin. Climb Gospel Pass, descend through Llanthony and rejoin main route at direction 28, where TL.

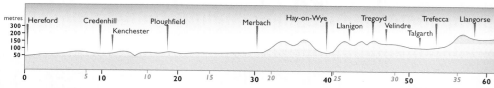

16 TL, SP Llanigon (still NCR).
38.5km (24 miles)

17 TL at TJ, SP Talgarth/Cycle Route 8 (cycle path on LHS). *48km (30 miles)*

18 TL at TJ. Immediately TR onto B4560, SP Llangorse/B4560. Continue on this road into Bwlch, passing access to Llangorse Lake on RHS.

19 TL at TJ, SP Abergavenny/A40.
62.5km (39 miles)

20 TR, SP Llangynidr. Cross River Usk.

21 TL at TJ onto B4558, SP Crickhowell. Continue through Llangynidr to Crickhowell (beside canal).

22 TL at XR, SP Crickhowell.
73km (45.5 miles)

23 TR at TJ, SP Abergavenny.

24 TL opposite castle ruins, SP Llangenny. TR at mini roundabout, no SP, and climb.

25 LHF, SP Partrishaw.
80km (49.5 miles)

26 RHF, SP Partrishow, and continue through Nature Reserve.

27 RHF, SP Llanthony. Then TR at TJ, SP Cwmyoy.

28 TR at TJ, SP Llanfihangel Crucorney (Cycle Route 42). *85km (53 miles)*

29 TL at TJ, SP Hereford, and again TL at TJ, SP Hereford, onto A465.

Brecon Beacons

30 To avoid climb, SO along A465 to Pontrilas and rejoin route at direction 31, where TL.

Otherwise, to continue main route, take first TR, SP Grosmont, and climb Campston Hill (excellent views). Pass access to Grosmont Castle on RHS and descend to TJ.

31 TR at TJ, SP Hereford/A465.
97km (60.5 miles)

32 TL in Pontrilas, SP Hay/B4348. Continue through Ewyas Harold, passing Dore Abbey on RHS.

33 TR, SP Wormbridge Kingstone. Pass Abbey Dore Court Gardens on RHS.

34 TL at TJ, SP Kingstone.

35 SO at XR, SP Hereford.

36 TR at XR, SP Hereford.

37 TR at TJ, SP Hereford/B4349.
112.5km (70 miles)

38 TL at TJ, SP Hereford.

39 SO at roundabout, SP Hereford. TL at roundabout, SP Town Centre, and cross River Wye. Arrive XR (traffic lights). Dismount and TR across road on foot, SP Cathedral. Join cycle path. Dismount at end of cycle path (opposite cathedral). TL and walk along Eign Gate pedestrian area. TR into High Street and along pedestrian area into High Town. LHF and continue to XR. Cross A438, SP Worcester. Remount and continue to station on LHS to complete the ride. *123.5km (77 miles)*

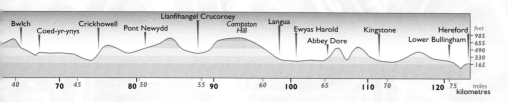

Places of interest along the route

A Hereford
A cathedral city on the River Wye. See route 23 for more details.

B Hay-on-Wye
A market town situated on the River Wye, famous for its second-hand and antiquarian bookshops and known as the Town of Books. See route 2 for more details.

C Llangorse Lake
The second largest lake in Wales, with a circumference of 6.5km (4 miles). A designated Site of Special Scientific Interest, the lake is surrounded by extensive reed beds, grassland and woodland, home to many different plants and animals, fish and birds. Free access at all reasonable times. Contact Crickhowell Tourist Information Centre for more details (see page 13).

D Crickhowell
Crickhowell sits on the River Usk and is dominated by Table Mountain (451m/1480 feet) to the north. See route 15 for more details.

E Grosmont Castle, near Grosmont
A castle is first thought to be have been built on this site during the 12th century and further building work took place during the 13th century. Cadw property. Contact Cadw for more information on (02920) 500200 or visit www.cadw.wales.gov.uk

F Dore Abbey, Abbey Dore
The abbey was founded by French monks in 1147, destroyed between 1536 and 1537 and restored during the 17th century. It is still used as a parish church. Visitors can see a wealth of stone and wood carving. Open all year, daily 0900–dusk. Donation requested. Telephone Hereford Tourist Information Centre for more details (see page 13) or visit www.doreabbey.org.uk

G Abbey Dore Court Gardens, Abbey Dore
A rambling 2.5ha (6 acre) garden and a nursery specialising in herbaceous perennials. Also licensed tearooms. Open April to September, daily (except Monday and Wednesday) 1100–1800; also open Bank Holiday Mondays. Charge. Telephone (01981) 240419.

H Llanthony Abbey, Llanthoney
Passed only if you take the shorter option over the Black Mountain. The abbey comprises the remains of an Augustinian priory in a remote setting in the Vale of Ewyas. Some of the abbey buildings have been incorporated into the Abbey Hotel.

Food and drink

Plenty of choice in Hereford, Hay-on-Wye and Crickhowell.

Neville Arms, Ewyas Harold
Meals available.

Abbey Hotel, Llanthony
Passed only on the shortened route. Hotel bar open Sunday–Thursday and Saturday, lunchtimes and evenings.

THE CTC
(Cyclists' Touring Club)

CTC is the UK's national cycling organisation. With seventy thousand members and affiliates, the club works for all twenty-two million cyclists in England, Wales, Scotland and Northern Ireland. CTC successfully lobbies on behalf of all cyclists and helped the government create its National Cycling Strategy. CTC also campaigns for improved countryside access, better cycling facilities on roads and at the workplace, and more space for bikes on public transport.

CTC provides essential services and invaluable advice for novice and experienced cyclists of all ages and abilities. It has 64 District Associations with 204 local groups plus hundreds of local campaigners in its Right to Ride network. New members and volunteers are always welcomed!

Cyclecover Insurance Services

CTC membership includes free third party insurance and legal aid. CTC also offers several cycling-specific insurance policies. Cyclecover Rescue is a unique twenty-four hour rescue scheme for cyclists stranded by breakdown (excluding punctures), accident, vandalism or theft. CTC offers annual travel insurance and single trip cover. Mountain biking, touring, repatriation of bike, luggage and accessory cover are all included. Comprehensive cycle insurance is offered to members and non-members alike, at very competitive premiums.

CycleSafe

Local authorities are being urged to sign up to four CycleSafe objectives, the aims of which are to improve safety for cyclists. That means reducing risks on roads, consideration for cyclists in new road layouts, adequate investment in cycling facilities and in cycling promotion. CTC has offered all authorities advice on engineering measures, education and examples of successful schemes elsewhere. In York, Britain's most cycling-friendly city, the implementation of a comfortable cycling environment has increased cycling by sixteen per cent and led to a ten per cent drop in cycling casualties in the last 20 years.

Technical and Touring Advice

CTC offers advice on buying a bike and other cycling equipment, maintenance and repair. CTC's events department has information on hundreds of routes both in the UK and abroad and experienced leaders run holidays to scores of destinations throughout the world. These tours are suitable for all cyclists ranging from families with young children to experienced distance riders.

rC Magazine

Cycle Touring and Campaigning is CTC's bi-monthly magazine which is free to members. Articles cover campaign news, tours, technical advice, event reports and equipment tests.

CTC Help Desk

Staff on the Help Desk answer queries on all things cycling, from contacts at your local group to the best route across the continent. The Help Desk can advise on travelling by train or bus with your bike, bike security and parking facilities in public places and on how to make the workplace more friendly to cyclists.

CTC Membership

Membership costs from just £15 per year. Whether you are a roadster, prefer the quiet of canal paths and the countryside, commute by bike or just enjoy a day out with the children, CTC is the essential accessory for you!

For more information contact the CTC Help Desk:
CTC, 69 Meadrow, Godalming, Surrey GU7 3HS
Telephone (01483) 417217
Fax (01483) 426994
Email helpdesk@ctc.org.uk
Website www.ctc.org.uk

Cyclecover Travel Insurance
For a quote or instant cover call the CTC Help Desk or visit www.cyclecover.co.uk

Cyclecover Rescue
Telephone free on 0800 212810.

Cyclecover Cycle Insurance
Telephone free on 0800 169 5798.

CycleSafe
Visit www.cyclesafe.org.uk

CTC Cymru

CTC Cymru (Wales) is the regional body which represents the CTC in Wales. It is active at local and national level, with a network of local groups across the country, and organises several events including the Welsh Festival of Cycling. CTC Cymru can be contacted at:
Room 118 Reardon Smith Building
UWIC Fairwater Campus
Fairwater
Cardiff
CF5 3XH
Telephone (02920) 553590
Or visit www.cyclewales.org.uk